Easy
Gluten-Free
Baking

Elizabeth Barbone

Easy Gluten-Free Baking

Elizabeth Barbone

LAKE ISLE PRESS NEW YORK

Published by:
Lake Isle Press, Inc.
16 West 32nd Street, Suite 10-B
New York, NY 10001
(212) 273-0796
E-mail: lakeisle@earthlink.net

Distributed to the trade by:
National Book Network, Inc.
4501 Forbes Boulevard, Suite 200
Lanham, MD 20706
1(800) 462-6420
www.nbnbooks.com

Library of Congress Control Number: 2008941772

ISBN-13: 978-1-891105-41-8
ISBN-10: 1-891105-41-8

Book and cover design: Liz Trovato

Editors: Katherine Trimble
        Stephanie White

This book is available at special sales discounts for bulk purchases as premiums or special editions, including customized covers. For more information, contact the publisher at (212) 273-0796 or by e-mail, lakeisle@earthlink.net

First edition
Printed in China

10 9 8 7 6 5 4 3 2 1

To Greg,
    with love.

Acknowledgments

The book you are holding in your hands is not the result of my work alone. This book has been touched, and made better, by many people.

Working with Lake Isle Press publisher Hiroko Kiiffner has been a joy-filled experience. From the start, Hiroko "got it." She understood my vision and allowed me to be myself on these pages. For that, I thank her.

Kate Trimble and Stephanie White are editors extraordinaire! They are unfailingly kind and utter professionals. Throughout this process, I have asked Kate and Stephanie countless questions and each question was answered and aided me in better understanding the complex process of putting a book together.

Tina Rupp brought her amazing eye for beauty to the photographs in this book. She perfectly captured the succulence of gluten-free baking. Watching Tina work was a privilege and more fun than I could have imagined.

Working alongside Tina was food stylist Toni Brogan. Although I don't think she had ever baked gluten-free before, she jumped into the project with enthusiasm and produced delicious looking food.

Prop stylist Stephanie Basralian selected lovely items that helped the food shine. In fact, the hardest part of the photo shoot was not sneaking off with any of her lovely linens.

Designer Liz Trovato wove my recipes and Tina's photographs into something lovely. Thank you!

Outside of this project, my work—and my life—have been aided by so many. When Maureen Murphy of Price Chopper approached me about teaching gluten-free classes for Price Chopper Supermarkets, I never could have imagined what a wonderful project it would turn into. Maureen and Gail Failing have been so fun to work and travel with! Meeting hundreds of students at each event is deeply rewarding.

Paula Gretzinger, Jessica Layton, Jason Gough, and everyone at WNYT have made live TV fun. Thanks for letting me spread the word about gluten-free baking!

None of this would be possible without the great support of my readers, members of glutenfreebaking.com, and my students. Thank you so much for sharing your stories with me, participating in class, and encouraging me. Your support means so much.

Paul DeMarco is my hair stylist but more importantly he is my friend. He has stayed late at work to do my hair before TV appearances more times than I can count. This makes my life easier and for that I can't thank him enough.

Over countless cups of Starbucks coffee, my dear friend Margaret Leathem has listened to the details of this project coming together. Her enthusiasm and support is a delight in my life.

Years ago, when I had the idea to start teaching gluten-free baking classes, Rita Brenenstuhl gave me the space to do it. Those small classes helped me find my teaching voice and reach out to the gluten-free community. Thanks "Aunt Rita" for believing in my vision and supporting me right from the start.

What would I do without Jessica Brearton? She is the sister that friendship, not family, gave me. Rarely a day goes by that I don't talk to Jess. There really are no words for how much Jessica means to me. So, I'll just say what we always say to each other: Thanks, buddy!

Lucky are daughters who have mothers who support them. I am a lucky one indeed! My mom has supported me in every area of my life. With her boundless energy and unceasing enthusiasm, my mom always makes my days brighter.

Greg Meuer, my husband and best friend, is my source of constant encouragement and support. It was Greg who first said, "I think you should write a cookbook." When I finally listened to his advice, he always believed in me, even when I didn't believe in myself. Thanks, honey! There is no one else with whom I would want to go through this adventure called life.

Contents

Introduction

Dear Gluten-Free Baker,

I'm guessing you've picked up this book because you are looking for easy gluten-free recipes. Look no further. That's exactly what you'll find!

Gluten-free baking can be overwhelming. If you've spent your life buying your bread, cookies, and cakes, the thought of having to bake can be frightening! Start with the basics: white bread, chocolate chip cookies, pancakes. When you begin with easy recipes that return favorite foods to your diet, living gluten free becomes much more enjoyable.

The recipes are laid out so that you'll feel comfortable baking gluten free. You won't find odd ingredients in my recipes. None of the recipes use bean flours or other exotic flours. I use rice flours, cornstarch, potato starch, and other easy-to-find ingredients. The only ingredient missing is the gluten. In addition, my recipes use real butter, sugar, eggs, milk, and cream. The results produce foods that no one will guess are gluten free.

My interest in gluten-free baking began when I was a pastry student at the Culinary Institute of America. While perusing the shelves of the library, I noticed a book titled *Against the Grain: The Slightly Eccentric Guide to Living Well Without Gluten or Wheat* by Jax Peters Lowell. This amazing book introduced me to the world of gluten-free living. I stayed up all night inhaling the text.

I don't have celiac disease, but I do have multiple severe food allergies. The upbeat manner in which Lowell talked about handling a dietary intolerance touched me to the core. Moreover, the gluten-free foods she so lovingly described intrigued me. I wanted to try them!

My measly student budget allowed me to buy only a few items: a loaf of bread, a brownie mix, and some premade cookies. With great anticipation, I headed back to my apartment to sample these treats. I was disappointed to say the least. Everything was dry and tasteless—and so expensive.

Although disenchanted with my gluten-free food experience, I was still curious. How would you bake good food without gluten? To me, it sounded like a fantastic challenge.

I began to experiment with gluten-free baking in my free time; I quizzed my instructors to find out what they knew about it and even did my internship at a gluten-free company. Simply put, I was in love with this new world of baking. My fellow students could not understand why I wanted to bake without gluten. It was hard to explain, but this way of baking felt right to me. I had found my passion.

After graduating from the Culinary Institute of America and then Mount Mary College, I decided to teach gluten-free baking classes using my own repertoire of recipes. My standard was (and still is!) to create gluten-free recipes that tasted just like their wheat counterparts, or as close as I could get. Since I'm not on a gluten-free diet, I make sure my gluten-free creations are put side by side with their gluten versions. They have to pass the test taste. If they don't, it's back to the kitchen.

I shared my recipes with the gluten-free community through classes and demonstrations. As the classes grew, students began asking for recipes they could share with their celiac friends and family members. It was then I decided to start a monthly gluten-free baking newsletter. I wanted it to be simple. No ads, just great recipes. Gluten-Free Baking and More, my monthly newsletter, was born in November of 2003. The newsletter has grown into a fantastic website, www.glutenfreebaking.com, with members from all over the globe. Soon after I began the newsletter, readers began asking for a cookbook. The book you are holding in your hands is the answer. I hope you enjoy it. Now, let's get baking!

—Happy gluten-free baking,

Elizabeth Barbone

Frequently Asked Questions

Why don't you use a gluten-free flour blend?

After testing numerous flour blends, I found them to be lacking. I had far superior results when I custom-blended flours and starches for a recipe. Breads require different flours than cookies. Cookies require different flours than cakes. The number one comment I hear about my recipes is that they taste just like wheat foods. I really believe this is because each recipe uses flours that are ideal for that recipe. If I ever create a "magic bullet" flour mix that works well in all recipes, I'll be sure to let you know!

Why are dry and wet ingredients listed separately in the recipes?

Dry and wet ingredients are separated to make preparing a recipe a little easier. Most of my recipes include the step: "In a bowl, whisk together dry ingredients." By having the dry ingredients in a separate column, you'll know right away which ingredients you need to whisk together.

I am a big advocate of preparing homemade mixes. They make life easier! The most time-consuming part of making a gluten-free recipe is often dragging out all the dry ingredients and measuring them. With a homemade mix, you've already done this work. When you need to make something, you can just grab a mix from your pantry, add the wet ingredients, and you're ready to go!

How do I make my own mixes?

When creating mixes, start with the recipes your family eats on a regular basis. There is no need to prepare mixes for recipes that you only make occasionally. Once you have a list of your favorites, decide how many mixes to create. If your family eats two loaves of bread per week, I recommend creating twelve bread mixes. That way, you won't have to think about measuring out a bread recipe for six weeks!

Before assembling your mixes, be sure to have all the necessary ingredients on hand. This is not the time to think, "Oh, I'll add that later!" If you do add the ingredient later, it will take additional time, defeating the purpose of using a mix. If you forget the ingredient, your recipe won't work!

Let's say you decide to create twelve mixes. Assemble twelve plastic bags and label, label, label! It's amazing how similar a bread mix can look to a cookie mix when the bag isn't labeled. Before filling the bags, write the date, recipe, and recipe source on the front of the bag with a permanent marker. By writing down the recipe source, you will know where to find the directions for completing the mix when you're ready to bake.

After labeling the bags, measure the ingredients directly into the bags. If the recipe calls for one cup of white rice flour, measure one cup of white rice flour into each of the bags you have assembled. Then move on to the next ingredient. By measuring one ingredient at a time, you leave less room for error. Don't measure all the ingredients into one large bowl and then divide among your bags. Gluten-free baking is sensitive. If the ingredients are not properly distributed, you might end up with too much xanthan gum in one bag and not enough in another.

Once you've measured the mixes, store them in a cool, dry place. They don't need to be stored in the refrigerator (unless they contain a high-fat flour like soy flour). Because flours absorb odors, be sure to store your mixes in an odor-free area, not next to the onions! Mixes can be stored for up to three months.

Why is sugar sometimes included under the wet ingredients?

Sugar is included in the wet ingredients when it needs to be creamed with the butter or added separately from the dry ingredients. If you are preparing homemade mixes and you'd like to measure your sugar in advance simply measure it into a small baggie. Place this baggie inside your homemade mix.

Why do I need to whisk the flours together in your recipes?

Whisking the flours together helps to evenly blend the ingredients and evenly distribute the xanthan gum, salt, baking powder, etc. It is an important step in the baking process. I recommend using a balloon whisk for this step. If you've made a mix, whisk the dry ingredients together after emptying your mix into a bowl.

Why don't all the recipes contain xanthan gum?

Xanthan gum, though I wouldn't call it a gluten replacement, does provide necessary structure for baked goods. Some baked goods, like bread and pizza, require a great deal of structure. Other foods, like cookies and pancakes, don't need it, so they are fine without xanthan gum.

Why don't the recipes contain bean flours?

I do not use any bean flour in my recipes. I don't like the taste or texture bean flours add to gluten-free baked goods. All of my recipes use a combination of gluten-free flours to provide you with the very best taste and texture.

The Basics: Ingredients, stocking your kitchen, appliances, and more!

Gluten-Free Baking Ingredients

White Rice Flour
This is made from ground rice from which the hulls, bran layers, and germ have been removed. It is pure white in color and sometimes grainy in texture. I prefer white rice flour from Asian food markets, as I find it has a smoother texture than other white rice flours.

Brown Rice Flour
This flour is ground rice with the bran still present. Brown rice flour has a slightly nutty flavor. It is available at health food stores and grocery stores.

Sweet Rice Flour
This flour is made from ground rice from sweet, "glutinous" rice. This flour provides a fine texture to baked goods and retains moisture better than regular white rice flour. It is excellent for baked goods like cookies and muffins but does not work well in yeast-raised breads. This flour is sometimes labeled "glutinous rice flour." It is available at Asian food markets and online.

Cornmeal
Cornmeal is ground whole corn. Cornmeal is available in grinds from coarse to fine. Don't confuse cornmeal with cornstarch!

Cornstarch
Cornstarch has a smooth texture, no flavor, and provides stability in gluten-free baked goods and sauces. Cornstarch is one ingredient that I don't buy at the Asian food market. I don't like the texture of Asian cornstarch (at least not the brands I have tried). At home and in the test kitchen, I use cornstarch that I pick up at the local grocery store.

Potato Starch
Made from cooked potatoes, potato starch lends a light and airy texture to baked goods. No strong potato flavor is present. To confuse gluten-free bakers, potato starch is often labeled "potato starch flour." Potato starch flour is potato starch and it is what you want to buy and use in recipes.

Potato Flour
Potato flour should never be confused with potato starch. Potato flour is made from dehydrated whole potatoes. It's heavy when baked and has a very distinct potato flavor. No recipes in this book use potato flour.

Sorghum Flour

Sorghum is a grass-like plant; when ground, it has a nutty flavor and adds protein to baked goods. Items baked with sorghum flour will have a creamy hue. Don't confuse sorghum flour with sorghum syrup, which is a molasses-like sweetener. Sorghum flour is available at health food and grocery stores.

Tapioca Starch (Flour)

Ground from the root of the cassava plant, tapioca starch provides structure to gluten-free baked goods. When tapioca starch is overused, a slimy or gummy texture can result. Tapioca starch is sometimes labeled "tapioca flour." Tapioca starch and tapioca flour are the same and can be found at health food and grocery stores.

Xanthan Gum

A necessary ingredient in gluten-free baking, xanthan gum is a derivative of corn sugar bacteria (yum!). It provides structure to baked goods, especially important in gluten-free bread baking. Some people detect a funny odor from xanthan gum. "Dirty socks" is how several of my students describe the odor. So, if you think your xanthan gum smells funny, it's still safe to bake with! (If you ever spill xanthan gum, don't use a wet rag or mop to clean the spill or you will be left with a sticky, slimy mess. To clean a xanthan gum spill, use a dry paper towel or, for a large spill, a handheld vacuum.) Xantham gum is available at health food and grocery stores.

Dried Sweet Dairy Whey

This ingredient is an essential for most of my gluten-free yeast bread recipes. While living in Milwaukee, I learned that the state of Wisconsin had a problem with too much whey. Whey is a byproduct of the cheese-making process. When two pounds of cheese is made, about thirteen to twenty pounds of whey remains! I learned that almost one-third of the milk proteins and all of the sugars are left in whey. I began to think whey might add needed protein, flavor, and color to gluten bread. The first time I used whey in gluten-free bread baking, the results shocked me. The bread had great color and a creamy flavor. I can't imagine baking gluten-free bread without it. Another benefit to using whey: it is very inexpensive. Always have this gluten-free miracle on-hand.

When shopping for whey, do not confuse it with "whey protein powders." For baking, you want pure sweet dairy whey. Check the ingredients label; the only ingredient listed should be whey, nothing else. Dried sweet dairy whey can be found at health food stores or purchased online.

Instant Nonfat Dry Milk

Nonfat dry milk is the most concentrated form of milk. With all of the water removed, dry milk powder has about 27% protein per cup, versus regular milk with about 3.25% protein per cup.

Do not confuse instant nonfat dry milk with energy drinks such as Carnation Instant Breakfast. Use only pure nonfat dry milk in your recipes. It is available at grocery stores.

Other Important Ingredients

Butter

I am a bit of a rogue baker when it comes to butter. I bake exclusively with salted butter. I find it brings more flavor to the recipe. Gluten-free flours tend to be a bit blah. The small amount of salt in salted butter boosts the flavor of baked goods. All the recipes in this book use salted butter for the best results. Margarine can be substituted in gluten-free baking, but will often affect the final product. I call for margarine in the recipes where it is interchangeable with butter.

Unless otherwise noted, butter should be at room temperature. To soften butter, you can leave it out on the counter overnight or you can use the microwave. When softening butter in the microwave, take care not to melt any of the butter. Each microwave is different. To perfectly soften butter in my microwave, I use a power setting of 30% and nuke it for ten seconds. By experimenting, you'll find the correct power setting and time to soften, but not melt, your butter. (Baking with melted butter will affect the texture of your final product—and not for the better! Melted butter doesn't hold onto air as room temperature butter does. Baking with melted butter will produce heavy cakes and cookies that spread. Always avoid baking with melted butter unless the recipe specifically calls for it.)

Dark Brown Sugar

Light brown sugar has no place in my kitchen. I use only dark brown sugar. The extra molasses content in dark brown sugar adds flavor and color to gluten-free cookies. When selecting your dark brown sugar, be sure the only ingredients are sugar and molasses. Try to avoid any dark brown sugar that includes "caramel color." Caramel color only adds color and doesn't bring any extra flavor to your baked goods.

Eggs

For best results, use large eggs with all of my recipes.

Milk

Unless milk type is specifically noted, any dairy milk can be used in these recipes. Using rice or soy milk may affect the final result.

Oil

I test my recipes using both corn and vegetable oil. Unless a specific oil is called for, use whatever liquid oil you prefer. (I don't recommend baking with olive oil. It has a strong flavor that will be present in your finished product.)

Stocking Your Gluten-Free Kitchen

You don't need to run out and buy everything on this list. This guide covers the basic ingredients for a gluten-free kitchen. Your personal tastes and eating habits should be your ultimate guide.

Flours
White rice flour, preferably from an Asian market
Brown rice flour
Sweet rice flour
Sorghum flour
Cornstarch
Potato starch
Tapioca starch

Homemade Gluten-Free Mixes
(To learn how to prepare homemade mixes,
    see page 13.)
Bread (see pages 68 through 78)
Pancakes (see pages 24 through 28)
Pizza (see pages 82 through 83)
Brownies (see page 134)
Classic Chocolate Chip Cookies (see page 91)

Sweeteners
Granulated sugar
Dark brown sugar
Honey
Molasses
Light corn syrup

Chocolate
Chocolate chips
Cocoa powder, preferably Dutch process
Unsweetened chocolate

Dried Fruits and Nuts
Dried cranberries
Dried cherries
Dried blueberries
Raisins
Assorted nuts (if you aren't allergic, of course!)

Pasta
Variety of gluten-free pastas

Produce
Onions
Garlic
Lemons

Canned Goods
Tomato products (diced tomatoes, tomato paste,
    tomato sauce)
Chicken broth
Vegetable broth
Beef broth
Beans
Pumpkin

Oils and Vinegars
Vegetable oil
Olive oil
Corn oil
Canola oil
Vinegars (balsamic and red wine are my favorites)

Spices and Herbs
Ground cinnamon
Ground nutmeg
Ground ginger
Ground cloves
Vanilla extract
Dried basil
Dried parsley
Dried oregano
Granulated garlic
Hot pepper flakes
Whole black peppercorns
Kosher salt
Iodized salt

In the Refrigerator
Eggs
Milk
Cheese (Parmesan, cheddar, mozzarella)
Butter

In the Freezer
Sliced homemade bread
Muffins/quick breads

Cookies (either prebaked or dough rolled
    into logs)
Pizza crust (baked, but not topped)
Cupcakes

Miscellaneous
Instant nonfat dry milk
Dried sweet dairy whey
Vegetable shortening

Essential Kitchen Tools

Using the correct tools in the kitchen is the same as using the correct tools in a workshop. You wouldn't use a hammer to screw a nail in place, would you? Selecting a few quality kitchen tools will make your gluten-free baking life much easier.

Measuring Cups and Spoons

To ensure baking success you must use a good set of measuring cups and spoons. For dry measuring, use stainless steel measuring cups. Look for a nested set that includes the standard $1/4$, $1/3$, $1/2$, and 1-cup capacity cups. Dry ingredients should be scooped into measuring cup and leveled to measure.

To measure liquid ingredients, the classic Pyrex measuring cup is ideal. I prefer 2-cup capacity liquid measuring cups.

In addition to two sets of measuring cups, you also need a set of measuring spoons. A stainless steel set that includes a $1/8$ teaspoon measure is my preference.

Whisk

My recipes instruct you to "whisk together dry ingredients." To do this you need a wire balloon whisk. Look for one with a handle that is easy for you to hold.

Cooling Racks

One of the keys to great baking is how you cool your baked goods. Placing your fresh-from-the oven creations on a wire cooling rack ensures that your bread does not become soggy and that your cookies stay crisp. I own ten cooling racks. I recommend having three in your home.

Mixing Bowls

You know you need a set of mixing bowls when you start putting ingredients for a recipe into one of your cereal bowls. Although I have several sets of mixing bowls ranging from ceramic to wood, I turn again and again to my melamine mixing bowls. Look for a set of three with a rubber ring on the bottom. This ring helps to keep the bowls from slipping on the countertop.

Basic Kitchen Tools to Have On Hand

Your favorite kitchen tools might vary. I think this list is a good place to start.

Dry and wet measuring cups and spoons

Mixing bowls

Wire whisks

Spatulas—both cake spatulas and rubber spatulas

New wooden spoons (old wooden spoons can hold onto gluten; it's best to discard your pre-celiac wooden spoons to avoid contamination)

Ball-bearing rolling pin

Assortment of scoops for cookies and muffins

Kitchen thermometer—preferably digital for testing bread temperatures

Oven thermometer (all ovens vary in temperature; for the best baking results, you need to know your exact oven temperature)

Parchment paper

Timer

Cookie pans

9x5-inch loaf pans for yeast breads and quick breads

12-cup muffin pan

8-inch round cake pans

Cooling racks

Kitchen Appliances

KitchenAid Stand Mixer

The KitchenAid stand mixer is an icon for a reason. It is the best on the market. For a gluten-free kitchen, it's a real blessing.

Do you need one? I want to shout, "Yes! Yes! Yes! Every gluten-free baker needs a KitchenAid!" But I am smart enough to know that this may not be true for everyone. I've never been in your kitchen and have no idea what your baking habits are like. Below is what I do know about KitchenAid mixers. I hope it helps you to decide whether you need one.

The Pros

Power. The mixing power of a stand mixer is about eight times stronger than a hand mixer. It can churn through double batches of cookie dough and bread dough with ease. You don't need to worry about burning out this motor. Having a mixer that can handle double batches is a huge time saver! Whatever you make, try making a double batch and freeze the other half. Soon your freezer will be stocked with great homemade goodies.

Speed. From slow to super fast and everything in between. Speed control is one of the reasons KitchenAid mixers can handle everything from the lightest meringue to the heaviest bread dough.

Endurance. If you hang around folks that bake long enough, the KitchenAid stories begin to emerge. "I've had mine for ten years." "I've had mine for twenty-five!" "My mother has had hers for forty years!" This mixer is an investment piece, but it is an investment that lasts.

Ease. Hand-free mixing doesn't sound like a big deal until you make a batch of bread dough with your hand mixer and realize you need to stand there for five minutes! You get bored and your hand gets tired. With a KitchenAid, you add all your ingredients to the bowl, turn on the mixer and walk away—something you can't do with a hand mixer!

Attachments. Did you know there are nineteen different attachments for a KitchenAid? You can equip the mixer with attachments such as a pasta maker or citrus juicer. Even though the mixer itself takes up space, it will save you space (and money) if you purchase the available attachments. (You can even get an ice cream maker bowl!)

The Cons

Storage space. KitchenAid mixers are heavy—about twenty-five pounds—and they can't be disassembled for easy storage. That means they need counter space. I don't recommend buying a KitchenAid if you can't store it in your kitchen. If you need to drag it out to use it, how practical is it? Instead, invest in a good hand mixer. (I love the KitchenAid Ultra Power Plus hand mixer. During one of my gluten-free baking weekends, it fell off the counter and hit the floor with a loud "thunk." I picked it up, cleaned it off, and it started with no problem!)

The price. At this time, a new KitchenAid mixer costs about $250. If you aren't ready to make that kind of investment, please don't; there is no need to go into debt for a mixer. However, watch local stores for sales. You can usually find great deals on a KitchenAid, especially during the wedding season.

Bread Machine

One of the questions I receive most often is, "Do I really need a bread machine?" Bread machines are a great fit for some bakers. For others, they become an appliance that just gathers dust. Your bread-baking and eating habits will determine whether you need a bread machine. Here are what I see as the pros and cons of bread machines.

The Pros

Time. The most important ingredient in a good loaf of bread is time. If you are pressed for time (who isn't?), bread machines are a nice investment. All you need to do is add the ingredients, press Start and walk away. About two hours later, you will have a loaf of bread. And, at the end of the baking process, you will only have one pan to clean. If you eat a loaf or more of bread a week, a bread machine might be a good investment.

No guesswork. If baking a loaf of bread makes you nervous, you will love a bread machine. You don't need to worry about mixing the dough or watching it until it doubles in size. I know many people who failed at bread baking until they used a bread machine.

Travel. One reader told me she takes her machine with her whenever she travels. While visiting family she is always ensured she has fresh bread, made in an uncontaminated environment.

Kid friendly. Celiac kids are amazing. They often handle the diet better than adults do. If your young celiac is interested in baking his or her own bread, a bread machine is a perfect partner. The ease of use allows young people to bake a loaf of bread on their own, with adult supervision, of course!

College friendly—usually. If your celiac son or daughter is headed to college, check with resident services and see if a bread machine is allowed in their dorm room. If a bread machine is allowed, mix up several resealable bags of homemade bread mix. Then a busy college student only needs to add yeast, water, eggs, and butter (or oil).

The Cons

Quality. Bread machines vary in quality from fantastic (Zojirushi) to poor (most other brands). Machines with a vertical rise pan and one mixing paddle just don't make great gluten-free bread. The only bread machine I recommend is the Zojirushi brand. A good bread machine will cost about $200. Inexpensive bread machines cause more frustration than they are worth. If you are going to buy a bread machine, you really need to make a financial investment.

The loaf. Bread machines only produce one style of bread: the loaf. If you bake mostly rolls or baguettes, a bread machine isn't right for you.

Food Processor

It slices. It dices. It chops. It shreds. It makes perfect piecrust. Does this sound like an infomercial for yet another useless kitchen gadget? It's not. These are just a few of the jobs a food processor can perform.

I LOVE my food processor. In tests, I have found you can make a batch of graham crackers in about two minutes (after measuring) with a food processor, versus eight minutes by hand. Ditto for the biscuits; a mere one minute with the food processor and seven and a half minutes by hand.

Why does a food processor perform these tasks so much faster than the traditional by hand method? The blade. Each of these recipes utilizes the "rubbing" technique. This technique is perfectly mimicked by the food processor. In fact, I would argue that it does it better than doing it by hand. When you "rub" butter (or solid shortening) into flour, you create layers of butter. These layers help baked goods to be tender and flaky. This method works best when the butter is very cold. When you rub butter into flour with your hands, the warmth of your hands softens the butter. Room temperature butter does not create the same layers as cold butter. Therefore, your finished product will not be as flaky. Using a food processor, the butter is incorporated into the flour very quickly, remaining cold.

In addition to producing flaky piecrusts and crackers, this appliance will also save you time in the kitchen. I wasn't kidding when I wrote that a food processor slices, dices, chops, and shreds. Depending on your model, you can purchase a wide variety of attachments for your food processor. You can slice an onion in about fifteen seconds, grate carrots in under a minute, and of course, make dough quickly. If you have a food processor, it's time to pull it out!

Breakfast

Traditional
Pancakes

These pancakes are light and fluffy—just as pancakes should be! And, this recipe does not require buttermilk, so you don't need to run to the store at the last minute for any special ingredients.

DRY INGREDIENTS
1/2 cup white rice flour
1/4 cup cornstarch
1/4 cup sweet rice flour
2 tablespoons granulated sugar
2 teaspoons baking powder
1/4 teaspoon salt

WET INGREDIENTS
1 large egg
1/2 cup milk
2 tablespoons vegetable oil, plus more for pan

Maple syrup, for serving
Butter, for serving

1. In a medium bowl, whisk together all ingredients. (You don't need an electric mixer for this batter.) Allow the batter to sit for 2 to 3 minutes before using.

2. Oil a griddle and heat over medium-high heat. Pour about 1/4 cup batter for each pancake onto griddle. Batter should sizzle when it hits the pan; if it doesn't, wait for it to heat a bit longer.

3. Flip pancakes when bubbles appear all over the surface of the pancake. Cook until golden brown, about another 1 1/2 minutes.

4. Serve at once with syrup and butter.

Serves 4

Baker's Note
Maple allergy? If maple is a no-no for you, try Lyle's Golden Syrup. This British import is pure cane sugar syrup. Light amber in color, it has a pleasant buttery caramel flavor and is superb on waffles and pancakes.

Blueberry
Pancakes

Fresh raspberries or blackberries also work very well in this recipe. Use whatever berry you love!

DRY INGREDIENTS
1/2 cup white rice flour
1/4 cup cornstarch
1/4 cup sweet rice flour
2 tablespoons granulated sugar
2 teaspoons baking powder
1/4 teaspoon salt

WET INGREDIENTS
1 large egg
1/2 cup milk
2 tablespoons vegetable oil, plus more for pan
1 cup fresh blueberries, washed and picked over to remove any sticks or stones

Maple syrup, for serving

1. In a medium bowl, whisk together dry and wet ingredients, except blueberries. (You don't need an electric mixer for this batter.) Allow the batter to sit for 2 to 3 minutes before using.

2. Oil a griddle and heat over medium-high heat. Pour about 1/4 cup batter per pancake onto griddle. Batter should sizzle when it hits the pan; if it doesn't, wait for it to heat a bit longer. Sprinkle about 1 tablespoon berries onto each pancake.

3. Flip pancakes when bubbles appear all over the surface of the pancake. Cook until pancakes are golden brown, an additional 1 to 1 1/2 minutes.

4. Serve at once with maple syrup.

Serves 4

Baker's Note
Feel like blueberry pancakes in the winter? Use frozen blueberries! They work really well in this recipe. Just be sure to allow the blueberries to thaw slightly before using.

Diner-Style Buttermilk Pancakes

There are pancakes and then there are diner-style pancakes. These are as big as a dinner plate, crunchy on the edges and fluffy in the middle. To make these pancakes at home, you'll need to cook them one at a time with lots of brown butter. (It's the brown butter that lends that wonderful crunchy exterior.)

DRY INGREDIENTS

1 1/2 cups white rice flour
1/2 cup cornstarch
2 tablespoons granulated sugar
1 teaspoon baking soda
1 teaspoon salt
1/4 teaspoon xanthan gum

WET INGREDIENTS

2 cups buttermilk
1/4 cup (1/2 stick) melted butter, plus room
     temperature butter for the pan
1 teaspoon vanilla extract
2 large eggs

Maple syrup, for serving

1. In a medium bowl, whisk together dry ingredients.

2. Add wet ingredients and stir batter until smooth. (Use either an electric mixer or a wooden spoon.) Allow the batter to sit for 5 minutes.

3. Meanwhile, heat an 8-inch nonstick skillet over medium-high heat. Melt about 1 tablespoon butter on the skillet until golden brown. Scoop about 1/2 cup batter into the pan. Pancake will bubble and set, about 2 to 3 minutes. Flip and cook an additional 2 to 3 minutes. Repeat, using additional butter for each pancake, until all the batter is used.

4. Serve at once with syrup.

Serves 4

Pumpkin Pancakes

My husband and I make pancakes each Sunday. In October, we pull out this recipe. These fluffy pancakes are resplendent with spices and are a fun—and easy—way to celebrate autumn!

DRY INGREDIENTS

1 1/2 cups white rice flour

1/2 cup cornstarch

2 tablespoons packed dark brown sugar

1 tablespoon baking powder

1 1/4 teaspoons pumpkin pie spice

1 teaspoon salt

1/4 teaspoon xanthan gum

WET INGREDIENTS

1 1/2 cups milk

3/4 cup pure pumpkin (not pumpkin pie filling)

1 large egg

2 tablespoons vegetable oil, plus more for griddle

Maple syrup, for serving

1. In a medium bowl, whisk together dry ingredients.

2. Add wet ingredients and blend until a batter forms. (Use high speed on a handheld mixer and medium-high on a stand mixer.)

3. Heat griddle over medium heat. Lightly grease the griddle with vegetable oil. Pour batter, about 1/4 cup each for generous pancakes, onto hot griddle. Batter should sizzle when it hits the griddle. If it doesn't, wait before adding more batter to the griddle. Cook pancakes until bubbles begin to pop and batter looks almost dry. Flip pancakes and cook until golden brown on both sides, about 1 to 2 minutes.

4. Serve with maple syrup. Any extra pancakes can be frozen, but do it as soon as they cool so they don't dry out.

Serves 4 to 5

Gingerbread Pancakes

One of the tastes I love most is gingerbread. While I love gingerbread cookies, moist, spicy gingerbread cake makes me swoon. These pancakes were inspired by cake gingerbread. Since this recipe requires many ingredients, I mix up the dry ingredients the night before I plan to make the pancakes. This way, I can wake up, make pancakes, and settle in with the paper.

DRY INGREDIENTS

1 cup white rice flour

1/4 cup cornstarch

2 tablespoons granulated sugar

1/2 teaspoon ground cinnamon

3/4 teaspoon ground ginger

1/8 teaspoon ground cloves

1/2 teaspoon salt

1 teaspoon baking powder

1/2 teaspoon baking soda

WET INGREDIENTS

2 tablespoons vegetable oil, plus more for griddle

1/4 cup unsulphered molasses

1 cup buttermilk

1 large egg

Maple syrup, for serving

1. In a large bowl, whisk together dry ingredients.

2. Add wet ingredients and blend until a batter forms.

3. Heat a griddle or large skillet over medium-high heat and lightly grease with vegetable oil or melted butter. Drop about 1/4 cup batter per pancake onto hot pan. Cook until bubbles appear all over the surface of the pancake, about 2 minutes. Flip and cook until golden brown, an additional 2 minutes.

4. Serve immediately with maple syrup.

Serves 4

Belgian Waffles

I am very particular about waffles. For me, a great waffle must have a crisp exterior and a soft, soufflé-like interior. To achieve this, let the waffles brown in the waffle iron.

DRY INGREDIENTS

1/2 cup white rice flour

1/4 cup cornstarch

1/4 cup sweet rice flour

1 teaspoon baking powder

1/2 teaspoon baking soda

1/2 teaspoon salt

1 teaspoon granulated sugar

WET INGREDIENTS

2 large eggs

1 1/2 cups buttermilk

2 tablespoons butter, melted

Gluten-free nonstick cooking spray

Maple syrup, for serving

1. In a medium bowl, whisk together dry ingredients.

2. In a small bowl, whisk together wet ingredients. Pour wet ingredients over dry ingredients. Blend until thoroughly combined.

3. Bake in waffle iron according to appliance instructions.

4. Serve immediately with maple syrup.

Makes 5 to 7 Belgian waffles

Baker's Note

These waffles can be made in a standard waffle iron or a Belgian waffle iron. Yield will vary depending on the size of the iron you use.

Spice
Waffles

These spice waffles are a nice change of pace from traditional waffles. I let them get nice and brown in the waffle iron. This way they are crispy on the outside and soufflé-like on the inside.

DRY INGREDIENTS

2 cups white rice flour

1/2 cup cornstarch

4 teaspoons baking powder

2 teaspoons ground cinnamon

1 teaspoon ground ginger

1/2 teaspoon ground nutmeg

WET INGREDIENTS

2 large eggs

1 1/2 cups milk

1/4 cup unsulphered molasses

1/4 cup vegetable oil

Gluten-free nonstick cooking spray

Maple syrup, for serving

1. In a large bowl, whisk together dry ingredients. Add wet ingredients. Blend batter until ingredients are thoroughly combined. Batter will be very thin.

2. Heat waffle iron according to manufacturer's directions. Grease hot waffle iron with cooking spray.

3. Pour about 2/3 cup batter for a standard iron onto prepared waffle iron. Cook about 3 to 4 minutes, or until golden brown and aromatic. Cook time will vary depending on the waffle maker.

Makes 12 to 14 standard waffles or 8 Belgian waffles

Chocolate Waffles

It's up to you to decide whether to serve these waffles for breakfast or for dessert. Either way, they're wonderful! For breakfast, serve with berries, syrup, and whipped cream. For dessert, serve with ice cream, chopped nuts, and a drizzle of caramel or chocolate sauce.

DRY INGREDIENTS

1 3/4 cups white rice flour
1/2 cup cornstarch
1/2 cup granulated sugar
1 tablespoon baking powder
3/4 teaspoon salt

WET INGREDIENTS

1 cup dark or semisweet chocolate chips, melted
3/4 cup (1 1/2 sticks) butter or margarine, melted
1 1/2 cups milk
3 large eggs
2 teaspoons vanilla extract

Gluten-free nonstick cooking spray

1. In a medium bowl, whisk together dry ingredients.

2. In a separate bowl, stir together melted chocolate and melted butter until well combined. Add milk, eggs, and vanilla. Whisk until smooth.

3. Add dry ingredients to chocolate mixture. Stir until thoroughly blended, about 30 seconds. The batter will be thin. Allow batter to stand for 10 minutes.

4. Heat waffle iron according to manufacturer's directions. Grease hot waffle iron with cooking spray.

5. Pour about 1/2 cup batter onto iron and bake 4 to 5 minutes. (The waffles will come out a bit soft. Don't worry! This is how they should be. Think of them as a cross between a waffle and a slice of cake!) Serve warm.

Makes 18 to 20 standard waffles or 8 to 10 Belgian waffles

French
Toast

Stale bread, eggs, and milk. It is amazing that these simple ingredients can make a spectacular breakfast! Try French toast with my cinnamon raisin bread.

6 slices day-old cinnamon raisin bread, sliced
 about 3/4 inch thick (see recipe, pages 75–76)
4 large eggs
1 cup milk
2 tablespoons vanilla extract
1/4 teaspoon ground nutmeg
1/4 teaspoon salt
1/4 cup (1/2 stick) butter

Maple syrup, for serving

1. Place bread in a single layer in a large baking dish.

2. In a small bowl, whisk together eggs, milk, vanilla, nutmeg, and salt. Pour egg mixture over bread. Soak bread for about 1 minute. Turn slices and soak another minute. (If bread looks dry, add more milk.)

3. Melt 2 tablespoons butter in a medium pan over medium heat. Remove 3 slices of bread from the baking dish, allowing excess egg to drip off into baking dish, and place in hot pan. Fry until golden brown, about 2 to 3 minutes per side. Repeat with remaining butter and bread.

4. Serve warm with maple syrup.

Serves 6

Baker's Note
This recipe is easily doubled or tripled. Slice an entire loaf of bread the day before you plan on making French toast for breakfast. Leave the bread uncovered on a baking sheet overnight. To keep it warm after cooking, heat oven to 250°F. Line a baking sheet with parchment paper and place in the oven. After cooking the French toast, transfer directly to the prepared baking sheet. Keep in the oven until you are ready to serve (no more than 1 hour).

Cinnamon Coffee Cake

This recipe made its debut in my Gluten-Free Breakfast Goodies class years ago. It has become a favorite of my students. Make it on a morning when you have time to linger with the paper, a thick slice of this coffee cake, and a great cup of coffee.

Vegetable shortening, for pan
White rice flour, for pan

For the Topping
1/2 cup packed dark brown sugar
2 tablespoons granulated sugar
3 tablespoons white rice flour
1 teaspoon ground cinnamon
3 tablespoons butter, softened

For the Cake
DRY INGREDIENTS
1 cup white rice flour
1/4 cup sweet rice flour
1/4 cup cornstarch
1 teaspoon baking soda
1 1/2 teaspoons baking powder
1 teaspoon xanthan gum
1/4 teaspoon salt

WET INGREDIENTS
1/2 cup (1 stick) butter, softened
1 cup granulated sugar
2 large eggs
1 cup sour cream

1. Preheat oven to 350°F. Grease and rice flour a 9x9-inch square pan.

2. Prepare the topping: In a small bowl, mix together all topping ingredients. Using a fork or your fingers, blend ingredients. (The ingredients should come together like damp sand.)

3. Prepare the cake: In a medium bowl, whisk together dry ingredients.

4. In a large bowl, cream butter and sugar together until light and fluffy. (Use high speed on a handheld mixer or medium-high speed on a stand mixer.) Add eggs, 1 at a time, mixing thoroughly between each addition. Add dry ingredients; mix until combined; batter will be dry. Add sour cream. Blend well until all ingredients are thoroughly combined, scraping down the sides of the bowl. Spoon batter into prepared pan. Sprinkle the topping over the top of the batter.

5. Bake for 35 to 45 minutes or until a knife inserted into the center of the pan comes out clean.

6. Cool pan on a wire rack. Cut cake into squares.

Serves 8

Almond
Coffee Cake

This recipe contains a fantastic almond streusel that adds a nice bit of sweetness and crunch to the cake.

Vegetable shortening, for pan
White rice flour, for pan

For the Streusel

1 cup packed dark brown sugar
1 cup sliced almonds
1/4 cup white rice flour
3 tablespoons butter, melted

For the Cake

DRY INGREDIENTS

11/4 cups brown rice flour
1/2 cup cornstarch
1/4 cup sweet rice flour
1 teaspoon baking powder
1 teaspoon baking soda
1 teaspoon xanthan gum

WET INGREDIENTS

1/2 cup (1 stick) butter, softened
1/2 cup granulated sugar
1 teaspoon vanilla extract
3 large eggs
2/3 cup orange juice

Glaze (optional) (see recipe, below)

1. Preheat oven to 350°F. Grease and rice flour a 12-cup Bundt pan.

2. Prepare the streusel: In a small bowl, stir together brown sugar, almonds, and white rice flour. Pour melted butter over the mixture and mix with a fork.

3. Prepare the cake: In a medium bowl, whisk together the dry ingredients. Set aside.

4. In a large bowl, cream together butter, sugar, and vanilla until light and fluffy. (Use high speed on a handheld mixer or medium-high speed on a stand mixer.) Add eggs, 1 at a time, mixing well between each addition. Add half of the dry ingredients; mix for 30 seconds. (Use medium-high speed with a handheld mixer or medium speed with a stand mixer.) Add half of the orange juice; mix for 30 seconds. Add remaining dry ingredients; mix for 30 seconds. Add remaining orange juice; mix for 1 minute.

5. Spread half of the batter into the prepared pan. Sprinkle half of the streusel mixture over the top. Spoon remaining batter over the streusel mixture. Sprinkle remaining streusel mixture over the batter.

6. Bake for 40 to 45 minutes or until a tester inserted into the center of the cake comes out clean.

7. Remove cake from oven and place on a wire rack to cool. Once cool, remove the cake from the pan. Glaze, if desired.

Serves 8 to 10

Glaze

1/2 cup confectioners' sugar
1 tablespoon orange juice

1. In a small bowl or cup, combine the confectioners' sugar and orange juice. Stir until smooth.

Sour Cream
Coffee Cake

Occasionally I am asked to do a cooking segment on our local news station. One day, I made this recipe for the show. After the program ended, the host kept asking me, "Is this really made without wheat? I can't believe it. I mean, really? No wheat?" I assured her that my coffee cake was indeed made without any wheat flour. When you make this cake for yourself or guests, I can assure you that you will have the same reaction.

For the Streusel
1/4 cup packed dark brown sugar
1 1/2 teaspoons ground cinnamon

For the Cake
Gluten-free nonstick cooking spray

DRY INGREDIENTS
1 1/4 cups white rice flour
3/4 cup cornstarch
1 teaspoon baking powder
1 teaspoon xanthan gum
1/2 teaspoon baking soda

WET INGREDIENTS
1 1/2 cups granulated sugar
3/4 cup (1 1/2 sticks) butter, softened
2 large eggs
1 teaspoon vanilla extract
1 cup sour cream

Confectioners' sugar, for sprinkling (optional)

1. Preheat oven to 350°F. Grease a 12-cup Bundt pan with cooking spray.

2. Prepare the streusel: In a small bowl, combine brown sugar and ground cinnamon.

3. Prepare the cake: In a medium bowl, whisk together dry ingredients. Set aside.

4. In a large bowl, cream together sugar and butter until light, about 30 seconds. (Use high speed on a handheld mixer or medium-high speed on a stand mixer.) Add eggs, 1 at a time, mixing until well combined. Reduce mixer speed to medium-low; add dry ingredients, vanilla, and sour cream; mix until a thick batter forms, about 45 seconds.

5. Spread one-third of the batter in the prepared pan. (Batter will be thick; use a spatula to spread it evenly.) Sprinkle streusel over the batter. Spread remaining batter over the streusel.

6. Bake cake for 55 minutes or until a tester inserted into the middle of the cake comes out clean.

7. Allow cake to cool in the pan 5 minutes then turn out onto a wire rack to cool completely.

8. Sift confectioners' sugar over the top of the cake, if desired.

Makes 1 Bundt cake

Granola

Do you miss granola? This easy-to-make granola is perfect for breakfast or a snack. Just be sure to use quinoa flakes, not quinoa flour!

4 cups quinoa flakes
1 1/2 cups sliced almonds
1/2 cup packed light brown sugar
1/2 teaspoon salt
1/2 teaspoon ground cinnamon

1/4 cup vegetable oil
1/4 cup honey
1 teaspoon vanilla extract
1 1/2 cups raisins or dried cranberries

1. Preheat oven to 375°F. Line a baking sheet with parchment paper.

2. Toss together all ingredients except raisins/cranberries.

3. Spread mixture evenly over baking sheet and bake, stirring every 15 minutes, about 45 minutes or until golden brown.

4. Remove pan from the oven and allow to cool on a wire rack.

5. When cool, stir in raisins/dried cranberries. Store in an airtight container.

Makes about 5 cups

Muffins and Quick Breads

Here's the good news about quick breads:

they're quick! In about 15 minutes you can have a quick bread in the oven. What is a quick bread? It's a muffin or loaf leavened with baking soda or baking powder.

Freshness Matters

Since quick breads depend on chemical leaveners for lift, make sure your baking soda or baking powder is fresh. Older baking soda or baking powders lose some of their leavening power, making for heavy quick breads.

Greasing the Pan

If you are baking your quick bread in a loaf or decorative pan, spray the pan generously with a gluten-free cooking spray or grease with solid vegetable shortening and dust with rice flour. Be sure to thoroughly coat the bottom and the sides of the pan to prevent sticking. If you are baking muffins, line your baking pan with paper liners.

Filling the Pan

Fill a loaf pan about two-thirds full. Most of my recipes, unless otherwise noted, will make one 9x5-inch loaf. If you are doubling the recipe to accommodate a decorative pan, be sure the pan is filled about two-thirds full. If you have any batter left, make a few muffins. Consider them a baker's treat!

Like loaves, muffin cups should be filled about two-thirds full. Any more batter than this will result in batter spilling all over your oven. (To easily fill muffin cups, I use a spring-release ice cream scoop.)

Cooling

Like any gluten-free baked good, quick breads should be cooled on a wire rack.

For loaves, allow the bread to cool in the pan for about five minutes. This will prevent the bread from falling apart. After five minutes, invert the bread onto a wire cooling rack. Tap the pan gently to loosen the bread and lift the pan slowly away from the bread. If the bread sticks, don't panic. Run a knife around the edges of the pan. Try to hold the knife close to the pan so you won't cut or dig into the loaf. Give the pan a firm shake to loosen the bread. Once the bread is free from the pan, turn it right side up and allow it to cool completely.

For muffins, allow the muffins to cool in the pan for two to three minutes. Then place the muffins directly on a wire rack to cool completely.

Freezing

Quick breads freeze wonderfully. Allow your muffins or loaves to cool completely before freezing. Wrap bread tightly with plastic wrap and then aluminum foil; store muffins in a freezer-safe plastic bag. Quick breads can be frozen for up to two months.

Wholesome Muffins

Egg-free and quick to make, these muffins have a pleasant graham-like flavor. I've been known to call them "whole-wheatless" muffins. They freeze very well and are perfect for mornings when you want something a little different for breakfast.

1 tablespoon flaxmeal (ground flax seeds)
2 tablespoons hot water

DRY INGREDIENTS
1 cup sorghum flour
3/4 cup brown rice flour
1/4 cup cornstarch
1/2 teaspoon xanthan gum
1 tablespoon baking powder
1/2 teaspoon salt
1/4 cup rice bran

WET INGREDIENTS
11/4 cups milk
1/4 cup vegetable oil
1/4 cup honey

1. Preheat oven to 350°F. Line a 12-cup muffin pan with paper liners.

2. In a small bowl, combine flaxmeal and hot water. Allow to sit for 8 to 10 minutes.

3. In a medium bowl, whisk together dry ingredients.

4. In a large bowl, stir together wet ingredients and flax mixture. Add dry ingredients and stir until thoroughly combined. (Use medium-high speed with a handheld mixer or medium speed with a stand mixer.)

5. Spoon batter into lined muffin cups, about two-thirds full. Bake for 18 to 20 minutes or until muffins are golden brown and spring back when touched.

6. Remove pan from oven and place on a wire rack to cool, 2 to 3 minutes. Remove muffins from pan and cool completely on rack. Store in an airtight container.

Makes 1 dozen muffins

Blueberry Muffins

While developing this recipe, I realized I forgot to buy a critical ingredient: blueberries! Annoyed, I ran to store to buy a bag of frozen blueberries. While there, I was delighted to find frozen wild blueberries. These tiny berries used to be a special treat for those of us lucky enough to sneak off to Maine during the summer. Their diminutive size makes them perfect for muffins. If you can find wild blueberries, use them. If not, regular blueberries work just fine.

DRY INGREDIENTS

1 cup white rice flour
1/2 cup sweet rice flour
1/4 cup cornstarch
1 tablespoon baking powder
1/2 teaspoon salt

WET INGREDIENTS

1/4 cup (1/2 stick) butter, softened
1/2 cup granulated sugar
1 large egg
3/4 cup milk

1 cup frozen blueberries, preferably wild
    Maine blueberries
1 tablespoon cornstarch

1. Preheat oven to 350°F. Line a 12-cup muffin pan with paper liners.

2. In a medium bowl, whisk together dry ingredients.

3. In a separate bowl, cream together butter and sugar until light and fluffy, about 1 minute. (Use high speed with a handheld mixer or medium-high speed with a stand mixer.) Add egg. Combine until thoroughly blended, about 1 minute. Add half the dry ingredients; mix until well combined (mixture will be dry). Add milk and combine. Add remaining dry ingredients and blend for 1 minute.

4. In a small bowl, coat blueberries with cornstarch. Fold blueberries into the batter.

5. Spoon batter into lined muffin pans, about two-thirds full. Bake for 15 to 20 minutes or until muffins are golden and spring back when touched.

6. Remove pan from oven and place on a wire rack to cool, 2 to 3 minutes. Remove muffins from pan and cool completely on rack. Store in an airtight container for 3 to 4 days, or freeze for up to 1 month.

Makes 1 dozen muffins

Coffee Cake Muffins

Sometimes I just want a little taste of coffee cake. For those times, these muffins are perfect. I can make a batch, eat one or two, and pop the rest into the freezer. Then, when the mood for coffee cake strikes again, all I need to do is defrost a muffin!

1/4 cup granulated sugar
1/2 teaspoon ground cinnamon

DRY INGREDIENTS
3/4 cup white rice flour
1/2 cup sweet rice flour
1/4 cup cornstarch
1/2 cup granulated sugar
2 teaspoons baking powder
1/2 teaspoon salt

WET INGREDIENTS
1 large egg
1/2 cup milk
1/4 cup vegetable oil

1. Preheat oven to 375°F. Line a 12-cup muffin pan with paper liners.

2. In a small bowl, stir together the sugar and cinnamon. Set aside.

3. Prepare the muffins: In a medium bowl, whisk together dry ingredients. Add wet ingredients and blend until smooth.

4. Fill prepared muffin pans about half full. Sprinkle about 1 teaspoon cinnamon-sugar mixture over each muffin. Top with batter to fill cups two-thirds full. Sprinkle an additional teaspoon of cinnamon-sugar mixture on top of each muffin.

5. Bake for 20 to 25 minutes or until golden brown.

6. Remove pan from the oven and place on a wire rack to cool, 2 to 3 minutes. Remove muffins from pan and cool completely on rack. Store in an airtight container.

Makes 1 dozen muffins

Morning Glory Muffins

I know, I know! The ingredient list for this recipe is longer than your arm. When several readers asked for a recipe for morning glory muffins, I hit the books. I had never heard of them. What I soon learned is that morning glory muffins could also be called "everything but the kitchen sink" muffins. The ingredient list is extensive. If you love a muffin full of all sorts of good tastes, this is for you.

DRY INGREDIENTS

1 3/4 cups white rice flour

1/2 cup cornstarch

1 1/4 cups granulated sugar

3 teaspoons ground cinnamon

2 teaspoons baking soda

1/2 teaspoon salt

1/2 teaspoon xanthan gum

WET INGREDIENTS

3 large eggs

3/4 cup unsweetened applesauce

1/2 cup vegetable oil

1 teaspoon vanilla extract

2 cups grated carrots

1 medium tart apple, peeled and grated (Granny Smith)

1 (8-ounce) can crushed pineapple, drained

1/2 cup sweetened, flaked coconut

1/2 cup raisins

1/2 cup chopped walnuts

1. Preheat oven to 350°F. Line two 12-cup muffin pans with paper liners.

2. In a large bowl, whisk together the dry ingredients.

3. In medium bowl, mix together the eggs, applesauce, oil, and vanilla. (Use medium-high speed with a handheld mixer or medium speed with a stand mixer.) Add the dry ingredients and continue to blend for 1 minute. Using a wooden spoon, stir in the carrots, apple, pineapple, coconut, raisins, and walnuts.

4. Spoon batter into prepared muffin cups so they are two-thirds full.

5. Bake for 35 minutes or until a tester inserted into the center of a muffin comes out clean.

6. Cool muffins in the pans for 5 minutes. Remove muffins from pans and cool completely on a wire rack. Store in an airtight container.

Makes 2 dozen muffins

Apple Cider Muffins

These muffins are inspired by the apple cider doughnuts that are so popular in my area. To ensure that the recipe has a nice cider flavor, make sure you use a good apple cider—preferably from a local orchard.

DRY INGREDIENTS

1 1/2 cups white rice flour

1/2 cup cornstarch

2 teaspoons baking powder

1 teaspoon salt

1 1/2 teaspoons ground cinnamon

1/4 teaspoon ground nutmeg

1/2 teaspoon xanthan gum

WET INGREDIENTS

1/2 cup (1 stick) butter, softened

3/4 cup packed dark brown sugar

2 large eggs

1 cup apple cider

1. Preheat oven to 350°F. Line 18 muffin cups with paper liners.

2. In a small bowl, whisk together dry ingredients.

3. In a large bowl, cream together butter and brown sugar; mix for about 1 minute until a thick paste forms. (Use medium speed with a handheld mixer or medium-high speed with a stand mixer.) Add eggs; combine thoroughly. Add dry ingredients and cider; blend, on medium speed, for 2 minutes.

4. Scoop batter into prepared muffin pans, filling them two-thirds full.

5. Bake for 25 to 30 minutes or until a tester inserted into the middle of the muffins comes out clean.

6. Remove pans from the oven and place on wire racks to cool, 2 to 3 minutes. Remove muffins from the pan and place directly on racks to cool completely. Store in an airtight container.

Makes 16 to 18 muffins

Jalapeño-Cheddar-Corn Muffins

These savory muffins are a great addition to almost any dinner.

DRY INGREDIENTS
2/3 cup white rice flour
1/3 cup cornstarch
1/4 cup sweet rice flour
1 cup cornmeal
2 tablespoons sugar
4 teaspoons baking powder
1/2 teaspoon salt

WET INGREDIENTS
1 large egg
1/4 cup vegetable oil
1 1/4 cups milk
1 cup grated cheddar cheese
2 jalapeño peppers, seeded and diced

1. Preheat oven to 350°F. Line a 12-cup muffin pan with paper liners.

2. In a medium bowl, whisk together dry ingredients.

3. In a small bowl, whisk together egg, vegetable oil, and milk. Pour egg mixture over the dry ingredients. Blend for 1 minute. (Use high speed with a handheld mixer or medium-high with a stand mixer.) Using a wooden spoon, stir in cheddar cheese and jalapeño peppers.

4. Spoon batter into muffin cups so they are two-thirds full.

5. Bake for 20 to 25 minutes or until a tester inserted into the center of a muffin comes out clean.

6. Place pan on a wire rack to cool, 2 to 3 minutes. Remove muffins from pan and place directly on rack to cool completely. Store in an airtight container.

Makes 1 dozen muffins

Garlic Muffins

I know some bakers don't like baking yeast breads. These garlic muffins were created for those folks. The garlic flavor is outstanding, and they're quick to prepare.

DRY INGREDIENTS

1 cup brown rice flour
1/2 cup white rice flour
1/2 cup potato starch
4 teaspoons baking powder
1 tablespoon granulated sugar
1/2 teaspoon salt

WET INGREDIENTS

1 cup milk
1 large egg
3 tablespoons butter, melted
1 tablespoon olive oil
1/2 cup grated Romano cheese, plus extra for sprinkling (or grated Parmesan cheese)
2 cloves garlic, minced (or more, to taste)

1. Preheat oven to 375°F. Line a 12-cup muffin pan with paper liners.

2. In a medium bowl, whisk together dry ingredients.

3. Add milk, egg, melted butter, and olive oil. Blend until smooth. (Use medium-low speed on a handheld or stand mixer.) Stir in grated cheese and minced garlic; mix until thoroughly combined.

4. Spoon batter into prepared muffin pans so they are about two-thirds full. Sprinkle about 1 teaspoon grated cheese over the top of the batter, if desired.

5. Bake for about 20 minutes or until light brown.

6. Place pan on a wire rack to cool, 2 to 3 minutes. Remove muffins from pan and place directly on rack to cool completely.

Makes 1 dozen muffins

Buttermilk Biscuits

As soon as the weather turns cool, I make buttermilk biscuits for dinner, usually as a side to roast chicken. Then for breakfast the next morning, I toast one (or two) and spread it thickly with jam.

DRY INGREDIENTS
2 1/4 cups white rice flour
1/2 cup cornstarch
1/4 cup sweet rice flour
2 tablespoons granulated sugar
4 teaspoons baking powder
1 teaspoon salt
1 teaspoon baking soda
1/2 teaspoon xanthan gum

WET INGREDIENTS
3/4 cup (1 1/2 sticks) chilled butter, cut into 1/4-inch pieces
1 1/4 cups buttermilk

1. Preheat oven to 425°F. Line a baking sheet with parchment paper.

2. In a large bowl, whisk together dry ingredients.

3. Using your fingers, rub the chilled butter into the dry ingredients until the mixture resembles a coarse meal. (No large pieces of butter should remain.)

4. Pour buttermilk over the mixture and stir until moistened.

5. Drop about 1/4 cup of dough for each biscuit onto the prepared baking sheet, spacing your biscuits about 2 inches apart.

6. Bake about 15 minutes or until biscuits are golden brown on top. Serve warm.

Makes 12 to 14 biscuits

Boston
Brown Bread

Brown bread is a traditional New England bread. It's not a yeast-raised bread; rather, it's a wonderfully dense quick bread. Classic recipes call for steaming the bread in a can or pudding mold for several hours. While my recipe uses ingredients found in the original steamed version, it is baked in a loaf pan. The taste is fantastic, and you can make it in half the time. This bread is traditionally served with cream cheese.

Vegetable shortening, for pan
White rice flour, for pan

DRY INGREDIENTS
3/4 cup sorghum flour
3/4 cup yellow cornmeal
1/2 cup brown rice flour
1/4 cup white rice flour
1/2 teaspoon xanthan gum
3/4 teaspoon baking soda
3/4 teaspoon salt

WET INGREDIENTS
1 1/2 cups buttermilk
1/2 cup unsulphered molasses

3/4 cup currants (optional)

1. Preheat oven to 325°F. Lightly grease and rice flour a 9x5-inch loaf pan.

2. In a medium bowl, whisk together the dry ingredients. Add the wet ingredients; mix until combined, about 30 seconds. (Use medium-high speed on a handheld mixer and medium on a stand mixer.) Stir the currants, if using, into the batter with a wooden spoon.

3. Spoon the batter into the prepared loaf pan and cover pan with a piece of greased aluminum foil. Fasten the foil tightly to the edges of the pan. This will allow the bread to steam.

4. Bake the bread for 45 minutes. Carefully remove the foil and bake the bread for an additional 10 minutes. (I got a small steam burn when removing the foil, so please be careful when peeling the foil off of the pan!)

5. Place pan on a wire rack to cool, 5 minutes. Remove bread from pan and allow to cool completely on rack.

Makes 1 loaf

Baker's Note
Don't be alarmed when you pull off the foil and see that the bread has only risen slightly. This is normal! Unlike other quick breads, Boston brown bread doesn't rise much. It's a dense bread, with an almost yeast-bread texture.

Blue Ribbon
Banana Bread

This banana bread is named after my mother's gluten-filled recipe. Her banana bread won several blue ribbons in bake-off contests. This gluten-free version will win you compliments.

Vegetable shortening, for pan
White rice flour, for pan

WET INGREDIENTS
1 cup granulated sugar
1 1/3 cups very ripe mashed bananas
1/2 cup (1 stick) butter, softened
2 large eggs

DRY INGREDIENTS
1 2/3 cups white rice flour
1/3 cup cornstarch
1 teaspoon baking powder
1 teaspoon baking soda
1 teaspoon salt
1/2 teaspoon xanthan gum

1. Preheat oven to 350°F. Grease and rice flour a 9x5-inch loaf pan. In a small bowl, mix together sugar and mashed bananas. Allow to sit for 15 minutes.

2. In a separate small bowl, whisk together dry ingredients.

3. In a large bowl, cream butter until light and fluffy. (Use high speed on a handheld mixer or medium-high speed on a stand mixer.) Add eggs, 1 at a time, mixing well between each addition. Add half of the dry ingredients. Blend until smooth. (Use medium speed on a handheld mixer or medium-low on a stand mixer.) Add banana-sugar mixture. Stir until well incorporated. Add remaining dry ingredients. Blend batter until smooth.

4. Pour batter into prepared loaf pan. Bake for 50 to 60 minutes, or until a tester inserted in the center of the cake comes out clean.

5. Place pan on a wire rack to cool, 5 minutes. Remove loaf from pan and place on rack to cool completely.

Makes 1 loaf

Skillet
Cornbread

There are countless recipes for cornbread, ranging from sweet cornbread muffins to savory cornbread with cheese and jalapeño. This recipe falls somewhere in the middle. Cooked in a skillet, it has a lovely, crunchy exterior and a moist flavorful interior. It is ideal for eating out of hand or alongside a hearty supper.

Gluten-free nonstick cooking spray, for skillet

DRY INGREDIENTS
1 1/4 cups cornmeal
1/4 cup white rice flour
1 tablespoon sugar
1 teaspoon baking soda
1/2 teaspoon salt
1/4 teaspoon xanthan gum

WET INGREDIENTS
1 1/2 cups buttermilk
2 large eggs
1/2 cup (1 stick) butter, melted

1. Preheat oven to 450°F. Spray an oven-safe 9-inch skillet with cooking spray. Place the skillet in the oven while the oven heats.

2. In a large bowl, whisk together dry ingredients.

3. In a medium bowl, whisk together wet ingredients. Pour over dry ingredients. Stir until well combined. (You don't need an electric mixer for this batter; a wooden spoon works just fine.)

4. Carefully remove the hot skillet from the oven and place it on a heatproof surface. Pour the batter into the skillet. Return the skillet to the oven and bake for 15 minutes, or until a tester inserted in the center of the cornbread comes out clean.

5. Remove the skillet from the oven and place on a wire rack to cool for 5 minutes. Turn cornbread out onto a serving platter. Cut into wedges and serve warm or at room temperature.

Serves 4 to 6

Cranberry
Bread

I love cranberries. However, if I was in the mood to make cranberry bread outside of cranberry season I was out of luck. One day I decided to try cranberry sauce in a recipe. It worked! The bread was full of cranberry flavor and, because cranberry sauce is available year-round, I can make it whenever the mood strikes.

Vegetable shortening, for pan
White rice flour, for pan

DRY INGREDIENTS
1 1/4 cups white rice flour
3/4 cup cornstarch
2 teaspoons baking powder
1 teaspoon ground cinnamon
1/2 teaspoon ground nutmeg
1/2 teaspoon xanthan gum

WET INGREDIENTS
1/2 cup (1 stick) butter or margarine, softened
1/2 cup granulated sugar
1 large egg
1 (16-ounce) can whole berry cranberry sauce
1 cup chopped walnuts (optional)

1. Preheat oven to 350°F. Grease and rice flour an 8x4-inch loaf pan. (A 9x5 loaf pan also works; the bread just won't be as high.)

2. In a medium bowl, whisk together dry ingredients.

3. In a large bowl, cream together the butter and sugar for 30 seconds. (Use medium-high speed with a handheld mixer or medium speed with a stand mixer.) Add the egg and combine. Add the dry ingredients and cranberry sauce. Mix until blended, about 45 seconds. Stir in walnuts if using.

4. Spoon batter into prepared loaf pan. Bake for 55 to 60 minutes or until a tester inserted into the center of the loaf comes out clean.

5. Place pan on a wire rack to cool, 5 minutes. Remove bread from pan and cool completely on rack.

Makes 1 loaf

Rosie's Perfect
Pumpkin Bread

I often receive letters and requests from readers wanting help making their family recipes gluten free. It brings me great joy when people can bake and share their favorite recipes with loved ones once again.

Vegetable shortening, for pans
White rice flour, for pans

DRY INGREDIENTS
2 1/2 cups white rice flour
1/2 cup cornstarch
5 teaspoons pumpkin pie spice
2 teaspoons baking soda
1 1/2 teaspoons salt
1 teaspoon xanthan gum

WET INGREDIENTS
4 large eggs
1 cup vegetable oil
1/2 cup orange juice
3 cups granulated sugar
1 (15-ounce) can pure pumpkin (not pumpkin
   pie filling)

1 cup dried cranberries (optional)

Dear Elizabeth,

I have tears in my eyes as I write this to you. You did it. You really did it. I can't believe I am eating my pumpkin bread again. The recipe is perfect. It is better than perfect. It is just like it used to be. Thank you a thousand times over. My family is thrilled. You have returned a tradition to my family and for that I can't thank you enough.

Rosie,
Massachusetts

1. Preheat the oven to 350°F. Grease and rice flour two 9x5-inch loaf pans.

2. In a large bowl, whisk together dry ingredients.

3. In a medium bowl, mix together eggs, oil, and orange juice. Add sugar and pumpkin. Blend until thoroughly combined. (Use medium-high speed on a handheld mixer and medium speed on a stand mixer.) Add pumpkin mixture to dry ingredients. Stir until all ingredients are thoroughly combined. Scrape bowl down once or twice while mixing ingredients. Stir in dried cranberries, if desired.

4. Pour batter into prepared pans. Bake for 1 hour or until a tester inserted into the center of the loaf comes out clean.

5. Place pans on a wire rack to cool, 10 minutes. Remove bread from the pans and allow to cool completely on a wire rack.

Makes 2 loaves

Irish Soda Bread

This version of Irish soda bread contains caraways seeds but don't feel like you need to include them in your recipe. If you don't like caraway, leave them out. The bread is wonderful either way.

Vegetable shortening, for pan
White rice flour, for pan

DRY INGREDIENTS
3 1/2 cups white rice flour
1/2 cup sweet rice flour
1/4 cup cornstarch
1/4 cup potato starch
5 teaspoons baking powder
1 1/2 teaspoons salt
1 teaspoon baking soda
1/2 teaspoon xanthan gum

WET INGREDIENTS
1 cup (2 sticks) butter, softened
2 large eggs
1 cup granulated sugar
2 cups buttermilk

1 tablespoon caraway seeds (optional)
1 1/2 cups raisins

1. Preheat oven to 350°F. Grease and rice flour a 9-inch springform pan.

2. In a medium bowl, whisk together dry ingredients.

3. In a large bowl, cream together butter, eggs, and sugar until light and fluffy, about 1 minute. (Use high speed on a handheld mixer or medium-high on a stand mixer.) Stir in half the dry ingredients. (Use low speed on a handheld or stand mixer.) Stir in the buttermilk until thoroughly combined. Add remaining dry ingredients and the caraway seeds and raisins; mix for 1 minute.

4. Pour batter into prepared pan and spread evenly. Bake about 1 1/2 hours or until a tester inserted into the center comes out clean.

5. Place pan on a wire rack to cool, 5 minutes. Remove bread from pan and allow to cool completely on rack.

Makes 1 loaf

Cheddar Dill
Bread

I like to think of this recipe as a biscuit–bread–quick-bread hybrid. It looks like a loaf of bread, is mixed like a biscuit and can be put together easily like a quick bread. While this bread is hard to categorize, it's easy to eat! Fragrant with dill and studded with cheddar cheese, this bread is excellent.

Gluten-free nonstick cooking spray

DRY INGREDIENTS

2 cups brown rice flour

1 cup white rice flour

1/2 cup cornstarch

1/4 cup potato starch

5 teaspoons baking powder

1/2 teaspoon dillweed

1/2 teaspoon salt

WET INGREDIENTS

1/3 cup cold butter

8 ounces sharp cheddar cheese, shredded

2 large eggs

1 1/2 cups milk

1. Preheat oven to 375°F. Spray a 9x5-inch loaf pan with cooking spray.

2. Place dry ingredients in the bowl of a food processor. Pulse a few times to thoroughly combine. (Don't have a food processor? See alternative directions, page 61.) Add butter and pulse until no large pieces of butter remain. (Mixture should resemble a coarse meal.) Add shredded cheese and pulse for 20 seconds or until cheese is evenly distributed.

3. In a small bowl, whisk together eggs and milk. Pour into food processor. Pulse until a batter forms.

4. Spoon batter into prepared pan. Bake 1 hour or until a tester inserted in the center of the loaf comes out clean.

5. Place pan on a wire rack to cool, 5 minutes. Remove bread from pan and allow to cool completely on rack.

Makes 1 loaf

Alternative directions:

1. In a large bowl, whisk together dry ingredients. Using a pastry cutter or your fingers, cut the butter into dry ingredients until no large pieces of butter remain. Mixture should resemble coarse meal.

2. Add shredded cheese. Blend until thoroughly combined. (Use low speed on a handheld or stand mixer.)

3. In a small bowl, whisk together eggs and milk. Pour mixture over dry ingredient/butter/cheese mixture and blend until a dough forms. (Use medium speed on a handheld mixer or medium-low speed on a stand mixer.)

Follow directions for baking on page 60.

Zucchini Bread

Zucchini bread, like fruitcake, has become something of a culinary joke. It seems folks assume you make zucchini bread only when your garden has produced too much of the vegetable. While this is a fine reason to make zucchini bread, I believe there is an even better reason: it tastes great!

Vegetable shortening, for pan
White rice flour, for pan

DRY INGREDIENTS
1¼ cups white rice flour
¼ cup cornstarch
¼ cup sweet rice flour
1 teaspoon baking powder
1 teaspoon baking soda
½ teaspoon salt
1 teaspoon ground cinnamon
½ teaspoon xanthan gum

WET INGREDIENTS
2 large eggs
½ cup vegetable oil
1 cup granulated sugar
1 teaspoon vanilla extract
1 cup grated zucchini

1. Preheat oven to 350°F. Grease and rice flour a 9x5-inch loaf pan.

2. In a medium bowl, whisk together dry ingredients.

3. In a large bowl, whisk eggs together with oil until well combined and slightly frothy. (Use high speed on a handheld mixer or medium-high on a stand mixer.) Add sugar and vanilla; mix until sugar is dissolved. Add dry ingredients and blend until thoroughly combined, about 1 minute. (Use medium speed on a hand-held mixer or medium-low on a stand mixer.) Using a wooden spoon, stir in grated zucchini. Pour batter into prepared pan.

4. Bake for 60 minutes or until a tester inserted into the middle of the loaf comes out clean.

5. Place pan on a wire rack to cool, 10 minutes. Remove bread from the pan and place on rack to cool completely.

Makes 1 loaf

Baker's Note
This recipe also makes fantastic muffins! Line muffin pans with paper liners. Fill muffin cups two-thirds full. Bake for 15 to 20 minutes or until a tester inserted into the center of a muffin comes out clean.

Makes about 2 dozen muffins

Yeast Breads

Yeast bread. It is one of the most challenging

baked goods to make gluten free. Notice I said challenging, not impossible. Get out your mixing bowl. It's time to make bread!

Water/Liquid Ingredients

The water used for making dough should be warm, not hot. Hot water, above 120°F, will kill the yeast. Use lukewarm water, about 110°F, to ensure healthy yeast growth.

Salt

The amount of salt in bread dough can seem quite small. There is generally only a teaspoon or two in an entire recipe. However, salt brings a great deal to bread dough. The salt helps to enhance flavor, control yeast growth, and provide structure. Forgetting to add the salt will result in bread that is flavorless and cottony in texture. One word of caution: Salt can kill yeast. When salt is in direct contact with yeast it will kill it. Never place the salt in the dough alone; always mix it with the flour or water before adding it to the dough.

Yeast

Yeast is a living organism. To make bread rise, which is yeast's job, yeast needs water and food. The yeast will feed on the starch found in the dough and produce carbon dioxide. I use active dry yeast in my bread recipes. Do not use rapid-rise yeast, which is formulated to make bread rise faster; I find it produces an inferior gluten-free bread.

Mixing

Since no gluten is present in gluten-free bread, people think it is not necessary to knead the dough. Although we are not developing gluten and no cohesive dough ball forms, I believe it is extremely important to knead (well, mix really) gluten-free dough for about five minutes. It helps to hydrate the flour and develop a smooth dough, and it increases the temperature of the dough, aiding the yeast. Although gluten-free bread dough might look mixed after only a minute or two, keep mixing! It makes a big difference.

Rising

When bread rises, fermentation is occurring. Fermentation produces important flavors, so don't rush the process. If you are not making bread in a bread machine, place your dough in a warm, draft-free environment to rise.

Baking

Bread needs to bake in a preheated oven. During the first five to seven minutes of baking, a phenomenon called oven spring occurs. When the yeast hits a hot oven, it goes into overproduction before it dies.

During this phase, the bread will rise. Therefore, it is very important that your oven is at the correct temperature.

Bread baking time will vary. I always found it hard to tell when gluten-free bread was done. To ensure it's thoroughly baked, take the bread's temperature. An internal temperature between 208°F and 211°F is ideal for gluten-free bread. This is slightly higher than the recommended 205°F temperature for wheat dough, but no raw spots occur. You'll want to use a good digital thermometer for this job. Test bread three-quarters of the way through baking. Remove the loaf from the oven and stab the thermometer in the middle of the loaf. Be sure not to touch the bottom of the pan, as this can skew the reading.

Cooling

Cooling is almost as important as baking. Allow your bread to cool on a wire rack. This will prevent soggy, gummy bread.

Freezing

Bread freezes wonderfully! Be sure to allow the loaf to cool completely before freezing. Slicing the bread prior to freezing is always a good idea. I like to slice my loaf and put two slices each into individual sandwich bags. This way I always have two slices ready to go for a sandwich. Do not refrigerate gluten-free bread; it will become soggy.

Using a KitchenAid to Make Bread

Use the flat paddle attachment, not the dough hook, for mixing gluten-free yeast bread. Place the mixed dry ingredients in the bowl, pour the wet ingredients (including the yeast) over the dry ingredients, and mix for five minutes on speed four to six. After five minutes of mixing, your bread dough should look smooth and slightly elastic.

Programming the Zojirushi Bread Machine

1. Select the homemade setting.

2. Set the preheat cycle for ten minutes.

3. Set the knead cycle for eighteen minutes.

4. Turn rises one and two off.

5. Set rise three for one hour.

6. Set the bake time for one hour and ten minutes.

7. Turn the "keep warm" cycle off.

Note: You can select your choice of crust settings, from light to dark. I think the dark setting produces the best crust on gluten-free bread.

The Zojirushi will remember the homemade setting. The next time you bake a loaf of bread, select the homemade setting and you will be ready to go. You will not have to reprogram the machine.

Baking Bread in the Zojirushi

1. Lock bread pan and mixers into the machine.

2. In a small bowl, mix together eggs, melted butter/oil, and water. Do not add the yeast.

3. Pour the mixture into the bread machine pan.

4. In a large bowl, whisk together all the dry ingredients. Add the dry ingredients to the bread machine.

5. Sprinkle the yeast on top of the dry ingredients.

6. Close the lid. Select the homemade setting and press Start.

7. The machine will beep a few minutes into the mixing. If you are adding any seeds, nuts, raisins, etc., this is the time to add them. If you are not adding any additional ingredients, ignore the beep.

8. Allow the machine to complete its cycle. Once the bread has finished baking, allow it to sit in the machine for 5 minutes. Then remove the bread from the machine and allow it to cool on a wire rack. If you let the bread stay in the pan any longer, it will become soggy and gummy.

Rye-Style Bread

I love Reuben sandwiches, and you need rye bread to make one. This recipe produces a deli-style "rye" bread.

Gluten-free nonstick cooking spray

WET INGREDIENTS
3/4 cup warm water (about 110°F)
1 packet (2 1/4 teaspoons) active dry yeast
1 cup warm, dark coffee (about 100°F)
2 tablespoons vegetable oil
2 large eggs
2 tablespoons dark unsulphured molasses

DRY INGREDIENTS
1 1/2 cups brown rice flour
1 cup sorghum flour
2/3 cup cornstarch
2/3 cup instant nonfat dry milk
1 tablespoon xanthan gum
1 tablespoon caraway seeds (optional)
1 teaspoon salt

1. Lightly grease a 9x5-inch loaf pan with cooking spray.

2. In a small bowl, combine water and yeast. Stir to combine.

3. In a medium bowl, whisk together dry ingredients. Add coffee, yeast mixture, oil, eggs, and molasses. Using a handheld or stand mixer, blend dough for 1 minute on low speed. Increase mixer speed to medium-high and mix dough for 5 minutes. (If you are using a stand mixer, use the flat paddle attachment.) Your dough should be soft, thick, and sticky. The dough will not form a cohesive ball. If you are using a handheld mixer the dough will try to climb the beaters; use a rubber spatula to push the dough back into the bowl. If the dough seems tight or dry, add another tablespoon of water and allow the dough to mix for 30 seconds to fully incorporate the additional water. At the right consistency, the dough should swirl delicately around the beaters. It shouldn't look dry, chunky, or dense; it should not be cake-batter thin, either. If the dough still looks dry, add another tablespoon of water.

4. Spread batter evenly into prepared pan. Lightly spray a piece of plastic wrap with cooking spray and cover the loaf lightly with plastic wrap. Allow dough to rise for 1 hour.

5. At least 15 minutes before the dough has finished rising, preheat oven to 350°F.

6. Remove plastic wrap and bake for 55 minutes or until internal temperature reaches 208°F to 211°F.

7. Remove bread from oven and allow it to cool in the pan for 5 minutes. Turn bread out onto a wire rack to cool completely.

Makes one 9x5-inch loaf

Easy Sandwich Bread

Not only is this sandwich bread really easy to make, it is delicious. It is perfect for sandwiches, bread crumbs, French toast, or any other recipe you make with bread! If you've never made gluten-free bread before, this is a great recipe to start with!

Gluten-free nonstick cooking spray

WET INGREDIENTS
1 3/4 cups warm water
1 packet (2 1/4 teaspoons) active dry yeast
2 tablespoons vegetable oil
2 large eggs

DRY INGREDIENTS
2 1/2 cups brown rice flour
2/3 cup cornstarch
2/3 cup instant nonfat dry milk
1 tablespoon xanthan gum
1 teaspoon salt

1. Lightly grease a 9x5-inch loaf pan with cooking spray.

2. In a small bowl, combine water and yeast.

3. In a medium bowl, whisk together dry ingredients. Add yeast mixture, oil, and eggs. Using an electric mixer, mix dough for 5 minutes on medium-high speed. (If using a stand mixer, use the flat paddle attachment.) Your dough should be soft, thick, and sticky. The dough will not form a cohesive ball. If you are using a handheld mixer the dough will try to climb the beaters; use a rubber spatula to push the dough back into the bowl. If the dough seems tight or dry, add another tablespoon of water and mix for 30 seconds to fully incorporate the additional water. At the right consistency, the dough should swirl delicately around the beaters. It shouldn't look dry, chunky, or dense; it should not be cake-batter thin, either. If the dough still looks dry, add another tablespoon of water to achieve the correct consistency.

4. Spread batter evenly into prepared pan. Lightly spray a piece of plastic wrap with cooking spray and cover the loaf lightly with plastic wrap. (If you cover the loaf tightly, the dough will have trouble rising.) Allow dough to rise for 1 hour.

5. At least 15 minutes before bread has finished rising, preheat oven to 350°F.

6. Remove plastic wrap and bake for 55 minutes or until internal temperature reaches 208°F to 211°F (use your digital thermometer about three-quarters of the way through baking). If the crust begins to get too dark before the internal temperature of the bread reaches 208°F, cover the loaf with a piece of aluminum foil.

7. Remove bread from oven and turn it out onto a wire rack to cool completely. Store at room temperature for 2 to 3 days, or slice and freeze.

Makes one 9x5-inch loaf

White Sandwich Bread

If I am known for one recipe, it would be this one. It makes a loaf of bread that is moist, toasts beautifully, freezes well, and has great flavor.

Gluten-free nonstick cooking spray

DRY INGREDIENTS

1 1/2 cups brown rice flour
1 cup white rice flour
1/3 cup potato starch
1/3 cup cornstarch
1/3 cup instant nonfat dry milk
1/3 cup dried sweet dairy whey
2 tablespoons packed dark brown sugar
1 1/2 teaspoons salt
4 1/2 teaspoons xanthan gum

WET INGREDIENTS

2 large eggs
1 3/4 cups warm water
1/4 cup (1/2 stick) butter, melted
1 packet (2 1/4 teaspoons) active dry yeast

1. Lightly grease a 9x5-inch loaf pan with cooking spray.

2. In a medium bowl, whisk together the dry ingredients.

3. In a large bowl, combine wet ingredients. Whisk together until yeast is dissolved, about 15 seconds. Add dry ingredients. Using a handheld or stand mixer, blend on low speed for 1 minute to thoroughly combine all ingredients. Increase mixer speed to medium-high and mix dough for 5 minutes. (If you are using a stand mixer, use the flat paddle attachment.) Your dough should be soft, thick, and sticky. The dough will not form a cohesive ball. If you are using a handheld mixer the dough will try to climb the beaters; use a rubber spatula to push the dough back into the bowl. If the dough seems tight or dry, add another tablespoon of water and mix for 30 seconds to fully incorporate the additional water. At the right consistency, the dough should swirl delicately around the beaters. It shouldn't look dry, chunky, or dense; it should not be cake-batter thin, either. If the dough still looks dry, add another tablespoon of water to achieve the correct consistency.

4. Turn the dough into prepared pan. Lightly spray a piece of plastic wrap with cooking spray and cover the loaf lightly with plastic wrap. (If you cover the loaf too tightly it will make it hard for the bread to rise.) Place pan in a warm, draft-free location and allow to rise for 1 hour. (On humid days, bread will rise faster.)

5. At least 15 minutes before the bread has finished rising, preheat the oven to 350°F.

6. Remove the plastic wrap from pan and bake for 1 hour or until the internal temperature of the bread reaches 208°F to 211°F (use your digital thermometer about three-quarters of the way through baking). If the crust begins to get too dark before the internal temperature of the bread reaches 208°F, cover the loaf with a piece of aluminum foil.

7. Turn the bread out onto a wire rack to cool completely. Store in an airtight container or freeze.

Makes one 9x5-inch loaf

Brown Sandwich Bread

This brown bread is a dark variation on my white sandwich bread. Like all of my recipes, it does not contain bean flours. Instead, I've used a combination of brown rice flour and sorghum flour to achieve a rich, whole-grain flavor. The coffee and molasses make the bread dark and flavorful.

Gluten-free nonstick cooking spray

DRY INGREDIENTS

2 cups brown rice flour

1/2 cup sorghum flour

1/3 cup potato starch

1/3 cup cornstarch

1/3 cup instant nonfat dry milk

1/3 cup dried sweet dairy whey

1 1/2 teaspoons salt

4 1/2 teaspoons xanthan gum

WET INGREDIENTS

2 large eggs

1 1/2 cups warm, strong, dark coffee

1/4 cup (1/2 stick) butter, melted

1 packet (2 1/4 teaspoons) active dry yeast

1/3 cup unsulphered molasses

1. Lightly grease a 9x5-inch loaf pan with cooking spray.

2. In a medium mixing bowl, whisk together dry ingredients.

3. In a large mixing bowl, combine eggs, coffee, butter, and yeast. Whisk together until yeast is dissolved, about 15 seconds. Add dry ingredients and molasses. Blend on low speed for 1 minute or until ingredients are thoroughly combined. Increase mixer speed to medium-high and mix dough for 5 minutes (If you are using a stand mixer, use the flat paddle attachment.) Your dough should be soft, thick, and sticky. The dough will not form a cohesive ball. If you are using a handheld mixer the dough will try to climb the beaters; use a rubber spatula to push the dough back into the bowl. If the dough seems tight or dry, add another tablespoon of water and mix for 30 seconds to fully incorporate the additional water. At the right consistency, the dough should swirl delicately around the beaters. It shouldn't look dry, chunky, or dense; it should not be cake-batter thin, either. If the dough still looks dry, add another tablespoon of water to achieve the correct consistency.

4. Spread dough evenly into prepared pan. Lightly spray a piece of plastic wrap with cooking spray and cover the loaf lightly with plastic wrap. Place pan in a warm, draft-free location and allow dough to rise for 1 hour.

5. At least 15 minutes before dough has finished rising, preheat oven to 350°F.

6. Remove plastic wrap from pan and bake for 1 hour or until the internal temperature of the bread reaches 208°F to 211°F. (Use your digital thermometer about three-quarters of the way through baking.)

7. Allow bread to cool in the pan for 5 minutes. After 5 minutes, turn bread out onto a wire rack to cool completely.

Makes one 9x5-inch loaf

Cinnamon Raisin
Bread

In this recipe the sorghum flour adds a hearty flavor that enhances the cinnamon and raisins. I love this bread toasted and spread with butter.

Gluten-free nonstick cooking spray

DRY INGREDIENTS

2 cups brown rice flour

1/2 cup sorghum flour

1/3 cup potato starch

1/3 cup cornstarch

1/3 cup dried sweet dairy whey

1/4 cup packed dark brown sugar

1 1/2 teaspoons salt

1 1/2 tablespoons xanthan gum

2 teaspoons ground cinnamon

WET INGREDIENTS

2 large eggs, at room temperature

1 3/4 cups warm milk (about 100°F)

1/4 cup (1/2 stick) butter, melted

2 teaspoons vanilla extract

1 packet (2 1/4 teaspoons) active dry yeast

1 cup raisins (see Baker's Note)

1. Lightly grease a 9x5-inch loaf pan with cooking spray.

2. In a medium bowl, whisk together dry ingredients.

3. In a large bowl, combine eggs, milk, butter, vanilla, and yeast. Whisk together until yeast is dissolved, about 15 seconds. Add dry ingredients and blend on low speed for 1 minute to thoroughly combine all ingredients.

4. Increase mixer speed to medium-high and mix dough for 5 minutes. (If you are using a stand mixer, use the flat paddle attachment.) Your dough should be soft, thick, and sticky. The dough will not form a cohesive ball. If you are using a handheld mixer the dough will try to climb the beaters; use a rubber spatula to push the dough back into the bowl. If the dough seems tight or dry, add another tablespoon of milk and mix for 30 seconds to fully incorporate the additional milk. At the right consistency, the dough should swirl delicately around the beaters. It shouldn't look dry, chunky, or dense; it should not be cake-batter thin, either. If the dough still looks dry, add another tablespoon of milk. Add raisins and mix for another 3 minutes.

5. Turn dough into prepared pan. Lightly spray a piece of plastic wrap with cooking spray and cover the loaf lightly with plastic wrap. Place pan in a warm, draft-free spot and allow to rise until doubled in size. Depending on where you live and your room temperature, this can take from 45 minutes to 1 1/2 hours.

6. At least 15 minutes before dough has finished rising, preheat oven to 350°F.

7. Remove plastic wrap from pan and bake for 1 hour or until the internal temperature of the bread reaches 208°F to 211°F (use your digital thermometer about three-quarters of the way through baking). If the top of the loaf gets too dark too quickly, cover the bread with a piece of aluminum foil and continue to bake.

8. Allow bread to cool in the pan for 5 minutes and then turn bread out onto a wire rack to cool completely.

Makes one 9x5-inch loaf

Baker's Note

If your raisins are soft and plump, you don't need to soak them; if they are dry and firm, then it is a good idea. To soak raisins, place in a bowl and cover with hot, but not boiling, water and allow to sit for about ten minutes. Drain the water and use the raisins as directed.

Hot Dog and Hamburger Buns

These buns are light, fluffy, easy-to-make, and hold up to a juicy hamburger or freshly grilled hot dog. I test my recipes thirty to forty times prior to publication. I think this recipe was tested twice that amount. I had very, very specific requirements for gluten-free hot dog/hamburger buns:

1. They needed to rise quickly. Who wants to spend all day making hot dog buns?

2. They needed to be light and moist.

3. They needed to complement, but never compete with the star of the show: the hot dog or hamburger.

4. They could not require special equipment. You don't need special rings or pans to make these buns.

DRY INGREDIENTS

1 1/2 cups brown rice flour

1 cup white rice flour

1/2 cup cornstarch

1 tablespoon xanthan gum

1 tablespoon sugar

1 teaspoon salt

WET INGREDIENTS

1 3/4 cups milk, at room temperature

1 tablespoon vegetable oil

1 large egg, at room temperature

1 packet (2 1/4 teaspoons) active dry yeast

Gluten-free nonstick cooking spray

1. In a large bowl, whisk together dry ingredients.

2. In a small bowl, combine wet ingredients. Whisk together until yeast is dissolved, about 15 seconds.

3. Pour wet ingredients over the dry ingredients. Blend with a handheld or stand mixer at medium speed, for 5 minutes.

4. Line a baking sheet with parchment. For hot dog buns, spoon the dough into oblong shapes about 5 inches long and 2 inches wide. For hamburger buns, spoon the dough into rounds about 3 inches across. Spray a piece of plastic wrap with cooking spray. Cover dough lightly with plastic wrap. Allow to rise in a warm place for 45 minutes.

5. At least 15 minutes before dough has finished rising, preheat oven to 350°F.

6. Remove plastic wrap and bake buns for 15 minutes or until golden brown.

7. Remove pan from the oven and transfer buns to a wire rack to cool completely.

Makes about 1 dozen rolls

Three-Seed Bread

Looking for a bread with more girth than sandwich bread? Sunflower, pumpkin, and flax seeds (along with sorghum flour) give this bread a nice hearty flavor without being too heavy.

I know this bread has a long list of ingredients. If you toast the seeds and measure out the dry ingredients the night before you plan to make the bread, the process will go very quickly!

Gluten-free nonstick cooking spray

Seed Mix
1/2 cup hulled, unsalted sunflower seeds
1/2 cup raw, unsalted pumpkin seeds
2 tablespoons flaxseeds

DRY INGREDIENTS
11/2 cups brown rice flour
11/2 cups sorghum flour
1/3 cup potato starch
1/3 cup cornstarch
1/3 cup instant nonfat dry milk powder
1/3 cup dried sweet dairy whey
2 tablespoons packed dark brown sugar
11/2 teaspoons salt
11/2 tablespoons xanthan gum

WET INGREDIENTS
2 large eggs
21/4 cups warm water (about 110°F)
1/4 cup (1/2 stick) butter, melted
1 packet (21/4 teaspoons) active dry yeast

1. Lightly grease a 9x5-inch loaf pan with cooking spray.

2. Combine seed mix in a dry frying pan. Toast seeds over medium heat, stirring constantly, until they begin to pop and become aromatic and golden brown. Remove seeds from pan and place in a heatproof bowl to cool.

3. In a large bowl, whisk together dry ingredients.

4. In a small bowl, whisk together wet ingredients. Allow to stand for 5 minutes. Pour wet ingredients over the dry ingredients and blend on low speed for 1 minute. Increase mixer speed to medium-high and mix dough for 5 minutes. (If you are using a stand mixer, use the flat paddle attachment.) Your dough should be soft, thick, and sticky. The dough will not form a cohesive ball. If you are using a handheld mixer the dough will try to climb the beaters; use a rubber spatula to push the dough back into the bowl. If the dough seems tight or dry, add another tablespoon of water and allow the dough to mix for 30 seconds to fully incorporate the additional water. At the right consistency, the dough should swirl delicately around the beaters. It shouldn't look dry, chunky, or dense; it should not be cake-batter thin, either. If the dough still looks dry, add another tablespoon of water. Add toasted seeds and mix for another 3 minutes.

5. Spread dough into a prepared pan. Lightly spray a piece of plastic wrap with cooking spray and cover the loaf lightly with plastic wrap. Place pan in a warm, draft-free location and allow dough to rise until double in size, 1 to 1 1/2 hours, depending on room temperature.

6. At least 15 minutes before dough has finished rising, preheat oven to 350°F.

7. Remove plastic wrap from pan and bake loaf for 1 hour or until the internal temperature of the bread reaches 208°F to 211°F.

8. Allow bread to cool in the pan for 5 minutes and then turn bread out onto a wire rack to cool completely.

Makes one 9x5-inch loaf

Snack Note

Toasted seeds are one of my favorite quick snacks. Remove hot seeds from the skillet and sprinkle generously with kosher salt and freshly ground black pepper.

If you aren't looking for a savory snack, omit the salt and pepper and add a handful of chocolate chips while the seeds are still warm. Stir to combine. The heat from the seeds will melt the chocolate. Once the seeds have cooled, add your favorite dried fruits.

Pizza

I'm not going to pretend making homemade pizza is as easy as calling your local pizzeria for takeout. But, if you follow these easy steps, it isn't burdensome. I promise!

Kneading

The simple joy of kneading bread dough is something many gluten-free bakers miss deeply. With this in mind, I set out to make a great-tasting pizza crust that could be kneaded by hand. I finally created a recipe that could be turned out onto the counter and kneaded. Kneading gluten-free dough is slightly different from kneading wheat-based dough. Here are two important steps to keep in mind:

- Rice flour your countertop, and your hands, generously. This will keep the dough from sticking. If the dough does stick, stop kneading and sprinkle rice flour onto the dough and your hands.
- Apply light to medium pressure on the dough ball. Remember, this is a gluten-free dough. You don't need to use a great deal of force. Lightly press the dough ball away from your body and then fold the dough onto itself. Continue for five minutes. This constant turning and folding will keep the dough in a ball. If you apply heavy pressure, the dough will flatten and might stick to the countertop.

Don't Feel the Need to Knead?

You don't have to knead the dough by hand. If you have a stand mixer, you can mix the dough, from start to finish, in a stand mixer. Follow recipe directions through step three. Instead of mixing the dough with a wooden spoon, mix the dough on low speed for about one minute. Add 1/4 cup additional white rice flour and turn the mixer to medium. Allow the dough to mix for 5 minutes. (I use the paddle attachment for this dough and all gluten-free yeast doughs.)

Rising

Pizza dough only takes about 45 minutes to rise. Be sure to cover the pan lightly with plastic wrap and a towel. Place the pan in a warm, draft-free environment.

Freezing Do's

Do freeze an unbaked crust. Roll the dough into the pan and cover with plastic wrap. Allow the dough to freeze for 24 hours. Remove dough from the pan and place on a cardboard circle. Wrap the crust tightly in plastic wrap and aluminum foil. Return dough to freezer. When you want pizza, remove the crust from the freezer. Place the unbaked crust (remember to remove the cardboard circle!) onto a lightly greased and cornmeal-floured baking pan and allow to thaw on the counter for three hours prior to baking. Bake and top as directed.

Do freeze a baked crust. (This is my favorite way to freeze pizza crust.) Follow the recipe directions through step seven. However, DO NOT top pizza. Cool baked crust(s) on a wire rack. When crust is completely cool, wrap with plastic wrap and aluminum foil. Freeze. When you want pizza, remove crust from freezer and remove wraps. Slide baked crust onto a lightly oiled and cornmeal-coated baking sheet. Allow crust to thaw for one hour prior to baking. Top and bake as directed.

Freezing Don'ts

Don't freeze pizza dough in a ball. Be sure to roll out the dough before freezing.
Don't top the pizza before freezing. Toppings don't freeze well, especially the cheese. Top your pizza just before baking.

Thick-Crust Pizza

DRY INGREDIENTS

1 1/2 cups white rice flour, plus more for dusting

1 cup brown rice flour

2/3 cup cornstarch

1/4 cup cornmeal, plus more for sprinkling

1/3 cup dried sweet dairy whey

1 1/2 teaspoons salt

3 tablespoons xanthan gum

WET INGREDIENTS

2 large eggs

1 1/2 cups warm water (about 110°F)

1/3 cup olive oil, plus more for pan

1 packet (2 1/4 teaspoons) active dry yeast

Gluten-free nonstick cooking spray

1. In a medium bowl, whisk together dry ingredients.

2. In a small bowl, whisk together wet ingredients.

3. Pour wet ingredients over dry ingredients. Stir to form a dough ball. (I use a wooden spoon.)

4. Turn dough onto a generously rice floured surface and knead for 5 minutes.

5. Lightly oil a 12-inch round pizza pan. Sprinkle cornmeal into the pan. Place dough in the pan and press the dough into the pan with your fingers, making sure the dough is even. Lightly spray a piece of plastic wrap with cooking spray and cover the pan lightly with plastic wrap. Allow the dough to rise for 45 minutes in a warm, draft-free environment.

6. At least 15 minutes before dough has finished rising, preheat oven to 475°F.

7. Remove plastic wrap from pan and bake dough, without topping, for 15 to 20 minutes or until crust is golden brown. Remove the pan from the oven, cover with sauce and cheese, and top with desired toppings. Return pizza to oven and bake until cheese melts and is golden brown and bubbling. (Sometimes I place the pizza under the broiler for a final blast to brown the cheese. It only takes a minute, so be sure to keep an eye on it.)

Makes one 12-inch pizza

Baker's Note

Don't have a 12-inch cake pan? You can bake your pizza in any 2-inch deep cake pan. The smaller the pan you use, the more pizzas you can make. Several of my students have invested in 6-inch cake pans. This small pan allows them to make personal pizzas for their family. Use whatever size pan you want. Just be sure not to overfill the pan. The pizza crust should not be more than 1/2 inch thick.

Thin-Crust Pizza

This pizza is so quick and easy to make, you'll find yourself turning to it again and again. It's thin and crunchy. Top it with whatever you love. For me, that means fresh tomato sauce, mozzarella cheese, caramelized onions, and kalamata olives.

DRY INGREDIENTS

1 1/2 cups brown rice flour

1 1/2 cups white rice flour, plus more for dusting

1/3 cup potato starch

1/3 cup cornstarch

3 tablespoons xanthan gum

1 1/2 teaspoons salt

WET INGREDIENTS

1/4 cup olive oil, plus more for pan

1 large egg

2 1/4 cups warm water (110°F)

1 packet (2 1/4 teaspoons) active dry yeast

Gluten-free nonstick cooking spray

1. In a medium bowl, whisk together dry ingredients.

2. In a small bowl, combine wet ingredients.

3. Add wet ingredients to dry ingredients. Using a stand mixer, mix dough on low speed for 1 minute. Turn mixer to medium-high and mix dough for 8 minutes; scrape down the sides of the bowl at least once during the mixing.

4. Lightly oil a 12x18-inch cookie sheet. On a lightly rice-floured surface, roll dough out into a large rectangle. Transfer dough to the cookie sheet. Press dough to fit the pan. Lightly spray a piece of plastic wrap with cooking spray and cover the pan lightly with plastic wrap. Allow dough to rise for 45 minutes in a warm, draft free environment.

5. At least 15 minutes before dough has finished rising, preheat oven to 425°F.

6. Remove plastic wrap from pan and bake dough, without topping, for 12 to 15 minutes.

7. Remove crust from the oven and immediately top with desired toppings.

8. Return pizza to oven and bake until cheese melts and is golden brown. Allow pizza to cool 3 to 5 minutes before cutting into pieces.

Serves 4 to 6

Quick Pizza Sauce

This uncooked sauce is really fresh tasting, and it's so easy to make. After the garlic has been cooked, hand the recipe off to your kids and let them finish making the sauce. It's that easy!

1 or 2 garlic cloves, crushed

2 tablespoons olive oil

1 (15-ounce) can crushed tomatoes

2 teaspoons dried basil

1/2 teaspoon dried oregano

3 tablespoons tomato paste

Crushed red pepper flakes, to taste

Salt and freshly ground black pepper, to taste

1. In a small skillet over medium heat, sweat the garlic in the olive oil until it becomes translucent. Be careful not to burn the garlic. Remove from heat.

2. In a medium bowl, combine garlic (with oil), tomatoes, herbs, and tomato paste. Stir to blend. Take care that the tomato paste mixes uniformly with the other ingredients. Season with red pepper flakes, salt, and black pepper to taste.

Makes about 1 1/2 cups

Really Quick
Pizza Sauce

2 tablespoons olive oil

1 (28-ounce or 32-ounce) can whole tomatoes, with juices

2 teaspoons kosher salt

1/4 teaspoon freshly ground black pepper

1. In a blender, combine all ingredients. Blend for 35 to 45 seconds or until sauce is almost smooth, as desired. (I like some chunks to remain. If you don't, blend the sauce longer.)

2. Store any unused sauce in the refrigerator for up to 3 days.

Makes about 3 cups

Caramelized
Onions

This is my favorite pizza topping. Allow the onions to cook long enough so they become brown and very soft; cooked this way, the onions take on a fabulous sweet flavor.

2 large yellow onions
2 tablespoons butter
2 tablespoons olive oil

1. Slice the onion into thin strips.

2. In a medium skillet over medium heat, melt the butter into the olive oil.

3. Add the sliced onions. Turn heat to low. Cook until onions soften and brown, 15 to 20 minutes, stirring frequently.

Makes about 1/2 cup

Cookies

So easy to make, so easy to eat! Whether you are making
chocolate chip cookies or lemon coolers, there are a few key steps to making perfect cookies.

Selecting the Pan

Before baking your cookies, you'll need to select a pan. It seems there are as many baking sheets as there are cookies themselves. I like to use a 13x18-inch heavy, rimmed aluminum pan. This is often referred to as a half sheet pan. I don't like cookie sheets without a lip around the sides. If you ever bake a cookie that spreads, there is nothing to stop the cookie from falling off the pan. When selecting a baking sheet, look for the heaviest pan you can get. Heavy pans are less likely to warp in the oven.

Lining the Baking Sheets

Thank goodness for parchment paper; it is essential for cookie baking. Simply place a piece of parchment on your baking sheet and you're ready to go. No need to spend time greasing the sheet or scrubbing off the greasy residue. Also, parchment paper helps cookies not to overspread.

The Creaming Method for Cookies

Creaming butter/shortening and sugar together when you make cookies is slightly different than when making cakes or muffins. If you whip the butter/shortening and sugar, air is incorporated in the butter/shortening and it will cause your cookies to spread. To properly cream ingredients for cookies use medium-low speed (unless the recipe specifies a different speed) and blend until a thick paste forms.

Rolling Cookies

Rolling gluten-free dough can be tricky. If the dough is too cold, it will crack. If it is too warm, it will stick to the counter. For dough to roll dough easily, you want it to be cool. I recommend removing your cookie dough from the refrigerator and allowing it to sit on your counter for about fifteen minutes. Then lightly rice flour your countertop and begin to roll. (Use a ball-bearing rolling pin.) There isn't a perfect thickness for cookies. The recipes will recommend a thickness, but that's just a recommendation. Roll cookies out however thick or thin you like.

After you've rolled the cookies, cut the dough using a lightly rice-floured cutter into whatever shape you desire. Try to cut the cookies as close together as you can to minimize the need to re-roll. Transfer cookies to your parchment-lined baking sheet with a spatula. Work any leftover scraps of dough into a ball. Wrap and chill for about 20 minutes, then re-roll. Gluten-free cookies won't get tough, so you can roll the dough as many times as you like. However, if you don't chill the dough, the cookies might spread.

Making Homemade Slice and Bake Cookies

Mix up a batch of your favorite cookies—chocolate chip and sugar cookies work extremely well. Divide the cookie dough in half. Place half the dough on a piece of parchment paper. Wrap the parchment around the dough to form a log. Twist the ends to seal and then wrap the entire log with aluminum foil. Repeat with remaining dough. When you are ready to make cookies, preheat the oven as directed. Slice the dough, from frozen, into 1/4-inch disks. Place disks onto a parchment-lined cookie sheet and bake.

I always recommend storing cookie dough in the freezer; it will keep there for up to two months. Due to the egg present in the dough, do not store cookie dough in the refrigerator for more than three days.

Drop Cookies

Use a cookie scoop! It makes the process go very quickly.

Baking

I bake one sheet of cookies at a time. This helps ensure even browning of all cookies. If you have an oven that bakes one side faster than the other, simply rotate the pan halfway through baking to avoid burning any cookies. To save time, line two cookie sheets with parchment paper. This way, as soon as one pan comes out of the oven, the other is ready to go in!

Unfortunately, cookies overbake quickly. The color of cookies is a good indicator of doneness. As the cookies begin to turn a golden brown, they are probably done.

Cooling

Gluten-free cookies are delicate. If you try to move the cookies to a wire rack right when they come out of the oven, they might break. Thankfully, it's easy to avoid this. After removing a tray of cookies from the oven, place the baking sheet on a wire rack for 3 to 5 minutes. Then transfer the cookies directly onto the wire rack to cool completely.

Freezing

Cookies freeze beautifully. Stack them in an airtight container, with a piece of parchment between the layers, and freeze for up to three months. Be sure to cool cookies completely before freezing.

Mailing Cookies

The best cookies to mail are drop cookies like chocolate chip, or cookie bars like brownies. Pack the cookies tightly into a plastic container or tin. Be sure to place a piece of parchment or waxed paper between the layers. Fill any gaps with a piece of balled-up parchment paper. Place the tin in a box large enough to hold it. Stuff the box with newspaper or packing peanuts. To ensure your cookies arrive fresh, use Express or Priority Mail.

Classic Chocolate Chip Cookies

Chocolate chip cookies have limitless variations. This recipe is inspired by the classic chocolate chip cookies made famous by Toll House.

DRY INGREDIENTS
11/4 cups white rice flour
1/2 cup sweet rice flour
1/4 cup cornstarch
1 teaspoon baking soda
1/2 teaspoon salt

WET INGREDIENTS
3/4 cup (11/2 sticks) butter, softened
1/4 cup granulated sugar
3/4 cup packed dark brown sugar
2 large eggs
2 teaspoons vanilla extract
1 (12-ounce) bag chocolate chips

1. Preheat oven to 350°F. Line 2 cookie sheets with parchment paper.

2. Whisk together dry ingredients.

3. In a large bowl, cream together butter, sugar, and brown sugar until a thick paste forms, about 1 minute. (Use medium speed on a handheld and stand mixer.) Add eggs, 1 at a time, mixing well between each addition. Add dry ingredients and vanilla; mix until a dough forms. Stir in chocolate chips with a wooden spoon.

4. Drop rounded tablespoonfuls of dough onto cookie sheets, about 2 inches apart.

5. Bake first sheet for 10 to 12 minutes or until golden brown.

6. Remove sheet from oven and place on a wire rack to cool, 3 to 5 minutes, then transfer cookies directly onto rack to cool completely. While first sheet is cooling, bake the second sheet of cookies. Store cookies in an airtight container.

Makes about 3 dozen cookies

Baker's Note
As written, this recipe will make Toll House-style cookies that flatten and spread a little during baking. If you like a cookie that stays in a mound, chill the dough for fifteen minutes prior to baking, and keep dough in the refrigerator in between batches.

Also pictured, Oatless Oatmeal Cookies, page 96.

Double Chocolate Chip Cookies

A delicious cross between a brownie and a cookie, this recipe is wonderfully rich and a chocolate lover's delight! The dough and baked cookies freeze well. Either freeze some dough balls and bake when you need a chocolate boost, or freeze a few cookies for a quick midnight snack.

DRY INGREDIENTS

1/2 cup white rice flour

1/4 cup cornstarch

1/4 teaspoon xanthan gum

1/4 teaspoon baking powder

1 (11-ounce) bag (13/4 cups) chocolate chunks

2 cups chopped nuts, if desired (walnuts, pecan, almonds, peanuts, or macadamia nuts)

WET INGREDIENTS

8 ounces semisweet chocolate, melted

1/2 cup packed dark brown sugar

1/4 cup (1/2 stick) butter, very soft

2 large eggs

2 teaspoons vanilla extract

1. Preheat oven to 350°F. Line 2 cookie sheets with parchment paper.

2. In a medium bowl, whisk together dry ingredients, except the chocolate chunks and nuts.

3. Pour melted chocolate into a large bowl. Add brown sugar, butter, eggs, and vanilla; mix until well blended, about 30 seconds. (Use medium-high speed on a handheld mixer; medium speed on a stand mixer.) Add dry ingredients; mix until well combined, about 45 seconds.

4. Using a wooden spoon, stir in chocolate chunks and nuts. (If you like your chocolate and nuts broken up into small pieces, use your mixer to incorporate these ingredients.)

5. Drop generous tablespoonfuls of dough about 2 inches apart onto prepared cookie sheets. Bake first sheet 12 to 14 minutes or until cookies are aromatic and dry in appearance.

6. Remove sheet from oven and place on a wire rack to cool, 3 to 5 minutes. Transfer cookies directly onto racks to cool completely. While the first sheet is cooling, bake the second sheet of cookies.

Makes about 30 cookies

Baker's Note

Love chocolate? Add 2 cups of white chocolate chips to this recipe, and, voilà, you've made triple chocolate chip cookies!

Peanut Butter
Cookies

These classic peanut butter cookies, complete with a crosshatch pattern, can be adapted to a peanut-free diet. If you have a peanut allergy, please see the allergy note below.

DRY INGREDIENTS

3/4 cup white rice flour
1/4 cup brown rice flour
1/4 cup sweet rice flour
1/2 teaspoon baking soda
1/2 teaspoon baking powder

WET INGREDIENTS

1/3 cup butter, softened
1/2 cup creamy peanut butter
3/4 cup packed dark brown sugar
1 large egg, at room temperature
1 teaspoon vanilla extract

1/2 cup granulated sugar

1. Preheat oven to 350°F. Line 2 cookie sheets with parchment paper.

2. In a small bowl, whisk together dry ingredients.

3. In a large bowl, cream butter, peanut butter, and brown sugar together. (Use high speed on a handheld mixer or medium-high on a stand mixer.) Add egg and vanilla; mix until thoroughly incorporated, about 30 seconds. Add dry ingredients. Blend until a dough forms.

4. Roll dough into balls, about 1 tablespoon each. Place the granulated sugar in a bowl. Roll dough balls in the sugar until coated. Place on prepared cookie sheets.

5. Lightly press the tines of a fork into the top of each cookie; press again to make a crosshatch pattern.

6. Bake one sheet of cookies for 10 to 12 minutes or until lightly brown.

7. Remove sheet from oven and place on wire racks to cool, 3 to 5 minutes. Transfer cookies directly onto racks to cool completely. While first sheet cools, bake the second sheet of cookies.

Makes 3 dozen cookies

Allergy Note
These cookies can be made with soy butter, sunflower butter, or golden pea butter. Simply replace the peanut butter with equal parts of your favorite peanut-free spread.

Baker's Note
Using your thumb, make an indentation in the center of each dough ball. Spoon in your favorite jam and bake. Please note: The jam will very hot when removed from the oven. Allow cookies to cool completely before serving.

Peanut Butter Chocolate Chip Cookies

While developing this recipe, I used my standard dark chocolate chips. I couldn't put my finger on what was missing from the recipe; nothing I did seemed to take the cookie from good to outstanding. Then one day I noticed a display in the grocery store for white chocolate Reese's peanut butter cups. "Yuck!" I thought. "No one will buy those! Peanut butter cups need to be milk chocolate and peanut butter." Then, it hit me. The peanut butter chocolate chip cookies should have milk chocolate chips, not dark chocolate chips! I finally had the cookies I was looking for.

(It turns out I was wrong about the white chocolate. Hershey's white chocolate peanut butter cups were so popular that they have become a permanent part of their product line. If you like the combination of white chocolate and peanut butter, try using white chocolate chips in this recipe.)

DRY INGREDIENTS

1 1/4 cups brown rice flour
1/2 cup cornstarch
1/4 cup sweet rice flour
1/4 teaspoon baking soda
1 teaspoon salt

WET INGREDIENTS

1 cup (2 sticks) butter, softened
1 cup packed dark brown sugar
1/3 cup dark corn syrup
2 large eggs
2 cups creamy peanut butter
2 teaspoons vanilla extract
3 cups (18 ounces) milk chocolate chips

1. Preheat oven to 325°F. Line 2 baking sheets with parchment paper.

2. In a medium bowl, whisk together dry ingredients.

3. In a large bowl, cream together the butter, brown sugar, and corn syrup, about 30 seconds. (Use medium speed on handheld and stand mixers.) Add eggs 1 at a time, blending well after each addition. Add the peanut butter and vanilla; mix until well combined, about 25 seconds. Stir in the dry ingredients and blend until thoroughly combined. Using a wooden spoon, stir in the chocolate chips.

4. Drop the dough by tablespoonfuls about 2 inches apart onto prepared baking sheets.

5. Bake the first sheet of cookies for 15 minutes or until they are light brown.

6. Place sheet on a wire rack to cool, 3 to 5 minutes, then transfer cookies directly onto rack to cool completely. While first sheet is cooling, bake second sheet of cookies.

Makes 5 to 6 dozen cookies

Oatmeal Cookies

With gluten-free oats on the market, I have received several requests for a gluten-free oatmeal cookie. I don't think anyone would guess this recipe is free of wheat!

DRY INGREDIENTS

3 cups gluten-free oats
1 cup white rice flour
1/4 cup cornstarch
1/4 cup sweet rice flour
1 teaspoon baking soda
1 teaspoon ground cinnamon
1/2 teaspoon salt

WET INGREDIENTS

3/4 cup (1 1/2 sticks) butter, softened
3/4 cup packed dark brown sugar
1/4 cup granulated sugar
2 large eggs
1 teaspoon vanilla extract
1 cup raisins (optional)

1. Preheat oven to 350°F. Line 2 baking sheets with parchment paper.

2. In a medium bowl, whisk together dry ingredients.

3. In a large bowl, cream together butter, brown sugar, and granulated sugar. (Use high speed on a hand-held mixer or medium-high on a stand mixer.) Add eggs, 1 at a time, mixing well between each addition. Add the vanilla. Reduce mixer speed to medium and add dry ingredients. Blend until a dough forms. Add raisins, if using. Cover dough and chill, 10 minutes.

4. Drop dough by tablespoonfuls onto prepared cookie sheets, about 2 inches apart.

5. Bake one sheet of cookies 10 to 12 minutes or until light brown and aromatic.

6. Remove cookie sheet from the oven and place on wire racks to cool, 3 to 5 minutes. Transfer cookies directly onto racks to cool completely. While first sheet is cooling, bake the second sheet of cookies.

Makes about 4 dozen cookies

Oatless Oatmeal Cookies

As I am sure you know, there is a great controversy surrounding oats. Some gluten-free eaters eat them; some don't. Whether you eat oats or not, you will love these cookies. By using quinoa flakes and chopped almonds, these cookies have a taste and texture very similar to traditional oatmeal cookies.

DRY INGREDIENTS

1/2 cup brown rice flour

1/2 cup white rice flour

1/4 cup cornstarch

1 teaspoon ground cinnamon

1 teaspoon baking soda

1 teaspoon xanthan gum

1/2 teaspoon salt

WET INGREDIENTS

1 cup (2 sticks) butter or margarine, softened

1/2 cup granulated sugar

3/4 cup packed dark brown sugar

2 large eggs

2 teaspoons vanilla extract

2 cups quinoa flakes

1 cup coarsely chopped almonds

1 cup raisins (optional)

1. Preheat oven to 350°F. Line 2 cookie sheets with parchment paper.

2. In a medium bowl, whisk dry ingredients together.

3. In large bowl, cream together butter and sugars, about 30 seconds. (Use medium speed on handheld and stand mixers.) Add eggs, 1 at a time, mixing well between additions. Add dry ingredients and vanilla. Blend until well combined. Turn the mixer to low and add quinoa flakes, almonds, and raisins, if using; mix well, about 45 seconds.

4. Drop dough by level tablespoonfuls onto prepared cookie sheets, spacing cookies 2 inches apart.

5. Bake one sheet of cookies 8 to 10 minutes or until lightly browned.

6. Remove cookies from the oven and place sheet on wire racks to cool, 3 to 5 minutes, then transfer cookies directly onto racks to cool completely. While first sheet is cooling, bake the second sheet of cookies.

Makes about 4 dozen cookies

Spritz Cookies

Over the years, I've had many requests for an easy recipe for spritz cookies. This recipe is wonderfully buttery with just a hint of almond flavor.

DRY INGREDIENTS
13/4 cups white rice flour
1/4 cup sweet rice flour
1/4 cup potato starch
1/2 teaspoon xanthan gum
1/2 teaspoon salt

WET INGREDIENTS
3/4 cup (11/2 sticks) butter, softened
2/3 cup granulated sugar
2 large eggs
2 teaspoons almond extract (or vanilla extract)
Food coloring, if desired

1. Preheat oven to 400°F. Line 2 cookie sheets with parchment paper.

2. In a medium bowl, whisk together dry ingredients.

3. In large bowl, combine butter, sugar, eggs, and almond extract. Cream together until light. (Use medium on a handheld mixer or medium-low speed on a stand mixer.) Add dry ingredients, mixing until a dough forms.

4. Divide and tint dough, if desired. (See Baker's Note.)

5. Fit a cookie press with desired template. Fill press with dough and squeeze out cookies, about 1 inch apart, onto prepared baking sheets.

6. Bake first sheet of cookies 8 to 14 minutes or until edges of cookies are very lightly browned. (Baking time depends on the size of the cookie your cookie press produces.)

7. Remove cookie sheet from the oven and place on wire racks to cool, 3 to 5 minutes. Transfer cookies directly onto racks to cool completely. While first sheet is cooling, bake second sheet of cookies.

Makes about 5 dozen cookies

Baker's Note
To color spritz cookie dough, divide dough according to how many colors you want to use, and place into separate mixing bowls. Using a spoon, stir in a few drops of food coloring. (Don't use a wooden spoon; food coloring can stain wood.) Remember, a little food coloring goes a long way; I usually start with 3 to 4 drops of food coloring for about 3/4 cup of dough and then add more color if needed.

Big Fat Cookies

Sitting among my hundreds of cookbooks is a worn, spiral-bound cookbook with a picture of hamburgers with olive eyes and pimento smiley faces on them. This cookbook, *Betty Crocker's Cookbook for Boys and Girls*, holds so many memories for me. It was my first real cookbook. I baked my way through some hits: cheesy pretzels, milk chocolate brownie cake, teddy bear paw cookies— and some misses: quick energy pickups, marshmallow custards, and peppermint taffy. But, again and again, I came back to Big Fat Cookies. It used a cake mix to create soft, cake-like cookies that were studded with chocolate chips.

A few months ago, I decided it was time for a gluten-free version of these cookies. Don't be put off by the long method. The recipe is easy and worth the effort! And get the kids involved in this recipe. It is a great memory maker.

DRY INGREDIENTS

2 cups white rice flour

1/2 cup cornstarch

1/2 cup sweet rice flour

11/2 teaspoons baking powder

3/4 teaspoon xanthan gum

3/4 teaspoon salt

WET INGREDIENTS

3/4 cup (11/2 sticks) butter or margarine,
    softened

11/2 cups granulated sugar

2 large eggs

3/4 cup milk

2 teaspoons vanilla extract

1/2 teaspoon almond extract

11/2 cups chocolate chips

1. Preheat oven to 350°F. Line 2 baking sheets with parchment paper.

2. In a small bowl, whisk together dry ingredients.

3. In a large bowl, cream together the butter and sugar, 1 minute. (Use medium speed on an electric stand mixer, or high speed on a handheld mixer.) Add the eggs 1 at a time, mixing well between each addition. After the last egg is added, mix for 30 seconds. Add half the dry ingredients to the butter-egg mixture. Blend for 30 seconds. Add half the milk and mix for 30 seconds. Add the remaining dry ingredients, milk, and extracts. Blend for 1 minute. Using a wooden spoon, stir in the chocolate chips.

4. Drop batter by the 1/4 cup onto prepared baking sheets, spacing cookies at least 2 inches apart. (Since these cookies are so big, I only bake 6 cookies per sheet.)

5. Bake first sheet of cookies for 10 minutes or until golden brown and puffy.

6. Remove cookie sheet from the oven and place on wire racks to cool, 3 to 5 minutes. Transfer cookies directly onto rack to cool completely. While first sheet cools, bake second sheet of cookies.

Makes about 2 dozen big, fat cookies

Lemon Coolers

Do you remember Schwan's? They're the company with the yellow trucks that deliver ice cream and other foods door-to-door. Years ago, they offered cookies called lemon coolers. These small, buttery cookies with a confectioners' sugar coating packed a big lemon punch. Schwan's no longer carries these cookies, but I never lost my taste for them. Here is a gluten-free version.

DRY INGREDIENTS

1 1/4 cups white rice flour
1/2 cup sweet rice flour
1/4 cup cornstarch
1/2 teaspoon xanthan gum
1 tablespoon lemon extract
Grated zest of 1 lemon

WET INGREDIENTS

1 cup (2 sticks) butter, softened
1/2 cup plus 1 pound confectioners' sugar
2 tablespoons freshly squeezed lemon juice

1. Preheat oven to 350°F. Line 2 baking sheets with parchment paper.

2. In a small bowl, whisk together dry ingredients.

3. In a medium bowl, cream together butter and 1/2 cup confectioners' sugar, about 30 seconds. (Use medium-high speed on a handheld mixer or medium speed on a stand mixer.) Add dry ingredients; mix 1 minute. Dough will be sandy. Add lemon juice and mix until a dough forms. If you are using a handheld mixer, this might take a minute or so. Cover dough with a piece of plastic wrap and chill for 1 hour.

4. Pinch off dough by the tablespoon and roll into balls (or use a cookie scoop). Place balls on prepared cookie sheets, about 1 inch apart.

5. Bake first sheet of cookies for 15 to 20 minutes or until lightly golden brown.

6. Meanwhile, fill a 9x13-inch pan with 1 pound confectioners' sugar.

7. Remove cookies from the oven. Place hot cookies directly into the confectioners' sugar. Bury the cookies so all surfaces are covered. Allow cookies to sit in the sugar for at least 2 hours or overnight. Bake second sheet of cookies after first sheet is in the confectioners' sugar. Shake off excess sugar before serving.

Makes about 3 dozen cookies

Homespun Sugar Cookies

For many, sugar cookies have come to mean cut-out cookies. But these are the opposite: They're soft, chewy and take far less time to make. The dough doesn't need to be chilled before baking—and they don't require a cutter. Cookies don't get any easier to make than this!

DRY INGREDIENTS

2 cups white rice flour
1/3 cup cornstarch
1/3 cup sweet rice flour
1/3 cup tapioca starch
1 teaspoon baking soda
1/2 teaspoon xanthan gum
1/2 teaspoon salt

WET INGREDIENTS

13/4 cups granulated sugar
1 cup (2 sticks) butter, softened
2 teaspoons vanilla extract
2 large eggs

Coarse sanding sugar

1. Preheat oven to 350°F. Line 2 baking sheets with parchment paper.

2. In a medium bowl, whisk together dry ingredients.

3. In a large bowl, cream together sugar, butter, and vanilla, about 1 minute. (Use medium speed on handheld and stand mixers.) Add eggs, 1 at a time, mixing until well combined. Reduce mixer speed to low and add the dry ingredients; mix 45 seconds.

4. Place the sanding sugar in a bowl. Roll dough into balls, about 2 tablespoons each. Roll each dough ball in the sanding sugar. Place coated dough balls onto prepared baking sheets, spacing cookies about 2 inches apart. Flatten cookies very slightly with your hands or a spatula.

5. Bake one sheet of cookies 12 to 15 minutes or until lightly golden brown.

6. Remove cookie sheet from the oven and place on wire racks to cool, 3 to 5 minutes. Transfer cookies directly onto racks to cool completely. While first sheet is cooling, bake the second sheet of cookies.

Makes about 2 dozen cookies

Baker's Note

Coarse sanding sugar adds a nice crunch and a lovely sparkly appearance to these cookies. Available in a wide variety of colors, it can be found in cake decorating shops or online. If you can't find sanding sugar, roll cookies in regular granulated sugar.

Jam Sandwich Cookies

These tender, buttery cookies are wonderful on their own, but get even better with a thin layer of jam holding two together.

DRY INGREDIENTS
2 1/2 cups white rice flour
1/2 cup cornstarch
1/4 cup sweet rice flour
2/3 cup granulated sugar

WET INGREDIENTS
1 cup (2 sticks) cold butter, cut into
    tablespoon-size pieces
1 large egg
3 tablespoons milk
2 teaspoons vanilla extract

1/2 cup jam, for sandwiching cookies together

1. Place dry ingredients in the bowl of a food processor; pulse a few times to combine. Add the butter and pulse until it is cut into small, pea-size pieces, about 20 seconds. Add egg, milk, and vanilla. Process mixture until a dough forms, 15 to 20 seconds.

2. Remove the dough from the processor and divide in half. Wrap dough rounds tightly with plastic wrap. Refrigerate for 4 hours or overnight.

3. Preheat oven to 350°F. Line 2 baking sheets with parchment paper.

4. Unwrap dough and allow it to sit on the counter for 5 minutes. Lightly rice flour countertop and roll out dough, about 1/8 inch thick. Use a 2-inch round cookie cutter and cut out cookies.

5. Place cookies on baking sheets and bake first sheet for 10 to 12 minutes or until cookie edges just begin to brown.

6. Remove cookie sheet from the oven and place on wire racks to cool, 3 to 5 minutes. Transfer cookies directly onto racks to cool completely. While first sheet is cooling, bake second sheet of cookies.

7. Sandwich cool cookies together using about 1/2 teaspoon jam for each sandwich.

Makes about 2 dozen sandwiches

Baker's Note

If you like peanut butter, spread one half of each sandwich cookie with peanut butter, the other half with jelly. Stick them together and you have peanut butter and jelly cookies!

For another fun variation, use a Linzer cookie cutter. Linzer cookie cutters are round cookie cutters with a cute mini-cutter in the center. Use the regular round cutter on half of the dough and the special cutter on the other half. When you sandwich these cookies together, jam will squeeze out of the cutout in the cookie.

New York Black and White Cookies

If you aren't from New York, you might not be familiar with my favorite cookie, the black and white cookie. The funny thing is, they aren't really cookies. They are more like individual cakes—about 5 inches across and iced on top with half chocolate and half vanilla icing. If you don't want huge, deli-size cookies, just use less batter per cookie than instructed.

DRY INGREDIENTS
2 cups white rice flour
1/2 cup cornstarch
1/2 cup sweet rice flour
11/2 teaspoons baking powder
3/4 teaspoon xanthan gum
3/4 teaspoon salt

WET INGREDIENTS
3/4 cup (11/2 sticks) butter or margarine, softened
11/2 cups granulated sugar
2 large eggs
3/4 cup milk
2 teaspoons vanilla extract
1/2 teaspoon lemon extract

1 (16-ounce) can gluten-free chocolate icing
1 (16-ounce) can gluten-free vanilla icing

1. Preheat oven to 350°F. Line 2 baking sheets with parchment paper.

2. In a small bowl, whisk together dry ingredients.

3. In a large bowl, cream together the butter and sugar, 1 minute. (Use high speed with a handheld mixer or medium speed with a stand mixer.) Add the eggs 1 at a time, mixing well between each addition. After the last egg is added, mix for 30 seconds. Add half the dry ingredients to the butter-egg mixture; blend for 30 seconds. Add half the milk and mix for 30 seconds. Add remaining dry ingredients, remaining milk, and extracts. Blend for 1 minute. Batter will be thick.

4. Use a 1/2-cup measuring cup to drop batter onto prepared baking sheets, spacing cookies about 3 inches apart. These cookies are very big and require a lot of room; you can only bake 4 at a time.

5. Bake first sheet of cookies for 20 to 25 minutes or until golden brown and puffy.

6. Remove cookie sheet from the oven and place on wire rack to cool, 3 to 5 minutes. Transfer cookies directly onto racks to cool completely. While first sheet cools, bake second sheet of cookies.

7. Spread white icing over half of the top of each cooled cookie and chocolate icing over other half.

Makes 1 dozen cookies

Baker's Note
To make life easier, I use store-bought icing on these cookies. If you have a favorite icing recipe you would rather use, go for it!

Jam Thumbprints

Since these cookies are so easy to make, I have a feeling they will soon be making a regular appearance in your kitchen. Use your favorite jam; I prefer raspberry.

DRY INGREDIENTS
2 1/4 cups white rice flour
1/2 cup sweet rice flour
1/4 cup cornstarch
1/2 teaspoon xanthan gum

WET INGREDIENTS
1 cup (2 sticks) butter, softened
2/3 cup granulated sugar
1 large egg
3 tablespoons milk

About 1/2 cup jam, any kind

1. Preheat oven to 350°F. Line 2 cookie sheets with parchment paper.

2. In a medium bowl, whisk together dry ingredients.

3. In a large bowl, cream together butter and sugar, about 1 minute. (Use medium speed on a handheld or stand mixer.) Add egg and blend for 30 seconds. Scrape down the sides of the bowl. Add the dry ingredients to the egg mixture; mix for 1 minute or until ingredients are thoroughly combined. Add milk and mix until combined. (Dough might be crumbly. Don't worry, it will roll nicely into balls.)

4. Roll dough into balls, about 1 tablespoon each. Place balls on prepared cookie sheets. Using your finger (or thumb) make a small depression in the center of each cookie. Spoon a small amount of jam into the impression.

5. Bake one sheet of cookies for 10 minutes or until lightly brown.

6. Remove cookie sheet from the oven and place on a wire rack to cool, 3 to 5 minutes. Transfer cookies directly onto racks to cool completely. While first sheet is cooling, bake the second sheet of cookies. (Resist the temptation to eat these cookies straight from the oven. The jam will be extremely hot and can burn!)

Makes 3 dozen cookies

Roll-Out Sugar Cookies

Christmas Butter Cookies

Gingerbread Men and Women

Almond Crescents

Gumdrop Cookies

Spice Drops

Santa's Whiskers

Holiday Cookies

Gimme a Kiss Cookies

Candy Cane Cookies

Eggnog Cookies

Pecan Tassies

Snowballs/Mexican Wedding Cookies

Chocolate Pixies

Molasses Crackle Cookies

No-Bake Peanut Butter Balls

Roll-Out Sugar Cookies

Holiday food rituals are so important. Sometimes folks on a special diet forget this. Although a gluten-free diet can be challenging, making homemade sugar cookies is not drudge-work. Pull out some cutters. Throw some rice flour on the counter and enjoy the ritual. That's what making holiday sugar cookies is all about.

DRY INGREDIENTS

2 1/2 cups white rice flour, plus more for dusting

1 cup sweet rice flour

1/2 cup cornstarch

1/2 teaspoon salt

1 1/2 teaspoons xanthan gum

WET INGREDIENTS

3/4 cup (1 1/2 sticks) butter, softened

1 1/2 cups granulated sugar

2 large eggs

2 teaspoons vanilla extract

1/4 cup water, as needed

Icing (optional)

1. In a small bowl, whisk together dry ingredients.

2. In a medium bowl, cream butter and sugar until light and fluffy. (Use medium speed on handheld and stand mixers.) Add eggs, 1 at a time, blending well after each addition. Add dry ingredients and vanilla; blend until a dough forms. (If a sandy mass forms instead of a dough ball, add 1/4 cup water and mix for 30 seconds. If the dough comes together on its own, omit the water from the recipe.)

3. Divide dough in half. Pat dough into rounds, wrap tightly with plastic wrap, and chill for 4 hours or overnight.

4. Preheat oven to 350°F. Remove dough from the refrigerator and allow to stand at room temperature for 15 minutes. Line two cookie sheets with parchment paper.

5. Generously dust a clean, dry work surface with rice flour. Roll dough about 1/4 inch thick. Using assorted cookie cutters, cut dough into desired shapes. Place cookies on prepared sheets.

6. Bake first sheet of cookies until lightly golden brown. (Baking time will vary depending on size of cookie.)

7. Remove cookie sheet from oven and cool on wire racks, 3 to 5 minutes. Transfer cookies directly onto racks to cool completely. While first sheet is cooling, bake second sheet of cookies.

8. Ice cooled cookies, if desired.

Yield will vary based on size of cookies; makes about 3 dozen 3-inch cookies

Christmas
Butter Cookies

DRY INGREDIENTS

1 1/2 cups white rice flour, plus more for dusting

1/2 cup sweet rice flour

1/2 cup cornstarch

1/2 teaspoon xanthan gum

1 1/2 teaspoons baking powder

WET INGREDIENTS

I cup (2 sticks) butter, softened

1 1/2 cups confectioners' sugar

1 large egg

1 teaspoon vanilla extract

1 egg white, lightly beaten (optional)

Sanding sugar, any color (optional)

Dear Elizabeth,

This is a recipe for Christmas cookies that my mother has made for as long as I can remember. Christmas at our house has always included these cookies and my daughter (now 21 years old) is making them. They are third-generation cookies! I was diagnosed with celiac disease this past January and realized that I wouldn't be able to enjoy them this year for the first time. If there is any way they could be converted, I would be forever grateful!

Thank you,
Mary G.,
Iowa

1. In a medium bowl, whisk together dry ingredients.

2. In a large bowl, cream together butter and confectioners' sugar, 30 seconds, on medium-high speed with handheld or stand mixer. Add egg and vanilla. Blend on medium speed, 45 seconds. Add dry ingredients and blend on medium speed, 1 minute.

3. Divide dough in half, pat into rounds, wrap tightly with plastic wrap, and chill for 4 hours or overnight.

4. Preheat oven to 350°F. Line 2 cookie sheets with parchment paper. Remove dough from the refrigerator. Allow it to sit on the counter for 10 minutes.

5. Lightly dust a work surface with rice flour. Roll dough about 1/8 inch thick. Using cookie cutters, cut into desired shapes. Place cookies on prepared baking sheets, about 1 inch apart.

6. If desired, lightly brush surface of cookies with egg white and generously sprinkle sanding sugar onto each cookie.

7. Bake first sheet of cookies until the edges are golden brown, about 10 minutes for 4x3-inch cutters (baking time will vary depending on the size of the cutters you use).

8. Remove cookie sheet from the oven and place on wire racks to cool, 3 to 5 minutes. Transfer cookies directly onto racks to cool completely. While first sheet is cooling, bake second sheet of cookies.

Yield will vary depending on the size of your cutters; makes about 3 dozen 3-inch cookies

Gingerbread Men and Women

These are quintessential gingerbread cookies. Once they are cooled, have some fun with the icing.

DRY INGREDIENTS

1 1/2 cups brown rice flour

1/2 cup white rice flour, plus more for dusting

1/2 cup sweet rice flour

1/4 cup cornstarch

1/2 tablespoon ground ginger

1 teaspoon ground cinnamon

1/4 teaspoon ground allspice

1 teaspoon xanthan gum

WET INGREDIENTS

1/2 cup vegetable shortening

1/4 cup water

3/4 cup unsulphured molasses

1/2 cup granulated sugar

Icing (optional)

1. In a large bowl, whisk together dry ingredients.

2. In a microwave-safe bowl, melt shortening in microwave (about 30 to 45 seconds on high power). Add water, molasses, and sugar. Stir well to combine.

3. Pour wet ingredients over dry ingredients. Blend for 2 minutes. (Use medium speed on handheld and stand mixers.) Dough will be stiff.

4. Divide dough in half. Pat dough into rounds and wrap tightly with plastic wrap; chill for 4 hours or overnight.

5. Preheat oven to 350°F. Remove dough from the refrigerator and allow to stand at room temperature for 15 minutes. Line two cookie sheets with parchment paper.

6. Dust a work surface generously with rice flour. Roll dough to about 1/4 inch thick. Cut into desired shapes.

7. Bake first sheet of cookies for 30 minutes or until golden brown and aromatic.

8. Remove cookie sheet from oven and cool on wire racks, 3 to 5 minutes. Transfer cookies directly onto racks to cool completely. While first sheet is cooling, bake second sheet of cookies.

9. Ice cooled cookies, if desired.

Yield will vary depending on the size of cookie cutters; makes about 3 1/2 dozen cookies using 4-inch cutters

Almond Crescents

These cookies are a classic of the holiday season: With their delicate almond flavor and powdered sugar that leaves a hint of a mustache, you can easily taste why!

DRY INGREDIENTS
1 1/2 cups white rice flour
1 cup ground almonds
3/4 cup cornstarch
1/4 cup sweet rice flour
2 tablespoons potato starch
1 teaspoon salt
1/4 teaspoon xanthan gum

WET INGREDIENTS
1 cup (2 sticks) butter, softened
3/4 cup granulated sugar
1 large egg
1 teaspoon vanilla extract
1 teaspoon almond extract

1 pound confectioners' sugar

1. In a medium bowl, whisk together dry ingredients.

2. In a large bowl, cream together butter and sugar until well combined, about 1 minute. (Use high speed on a handheld mixer and medium-high speed on a stand mixer.) Add the egg, vanilla, and almond extract; mix for 30 seconds. Reduce mixer speed to medium-low and add dry ingredients; blend until a dough forms.

3. Press plastic wrap directly onto dough and chill in the bowl, 30 minutes.

4. Preheat oven to 350°F. Line 2 baking sheets with parchment paper.

5. Pinch off about 2 teaspoons dough per cookie and roll into ropes; shape ropes into crescents. Place crescents on prepared cookie sheets.

6. Bake first sheet for 15 to 18 minutes or until lightly golden brown.

7. Meanwhile, fill a baking pan with 1 pound confectioners' sugar.

8. Remove cookie sheet from the oven and place on wire racks to cool, 1 minute. While first sheet cools, bake second sheet of cookies.

9. Place cookies in confectioners' sugar. Bury cookies so all surfaces are covered. Allow cookies to sit in the confectioners' sugar for 2 hours.

10. Roll each cookie in the confectioners' sugar and then shake to remove excess sugar.

Makes about 3 1/2 dozen cookies

Gumdrop Cookies

DRY INGREDIENTS

1 1/2 cups white rice flour

1/2 cup cornstarch

1 1/2 teaspoons ground cinnamon

1/4 teaspoon baking soda

1/4 teaspoon salt

1/4 teaspoon xanthan gum

WET INGREDIENTS

1/2 cup (1 stick) butter, softened

1 cup packed dark brown sugar

2 large eggs

1/4 cup sour cream

1 1/2 cups small gumdrops, halved (I used spiced gumdrops. But any kind will work, and taste, just fine.)

Dear Elizabeth,

My family has been great helping me adapt to the gluten-free diet. Our entire house is gluten-free and no one (usually) complains. However, last Christmas my son and daughter were lamenting the loss of their beloved gumdrop cookies. As a family project, we would spend an afternoon making these cookies. My husband was in charge of chopping the gumdrops (which are hard to chop!), and the kids would help me measure and drop the dough onto the cookie pan. I was in charge of watching the cookies so they didn't burn. My family would be so happy if you could make this recipe gluten free. Thank you.

Christine W.
Oregon

1. Preheat oven to 350°F. Line 2 cookie sheets with parchment paper.

2. Whisk together dry ingredients in a small bowl.

3. In a medium bowl, cream together butter and sugar, about 1 minute. (Use medium-high with a handheld mixer, medium speed with a stand mixer.) Scrape down the sides of the mixing bowl. Add eggs and beat until well combined. Reduce mixer speed to medium for handheld mixer, medium/low for stand mixer and add dry ingredients; mix for 45 seconds. Add sour cream and blend, 30 seconds. Add chopped gumdrops and stir until combined.

4. Drop dough by the tablespoonful onto prepared cookie sheets, spacing cookies about 2 inches apart.

5. Bake first sheet of cookies 15 to 18 minutes or until edges are light brown.

6. Remove cookie sheet from oven and place on wire racks to cool, 3 to 5 minutes. Transfer cookies directly to racks to cool completely. While first sheet cools, bake second sheet of cookies.

Makes about 4 1/2 dozen cookies

Baker's Note
Gumdrops are hard to chop! They love to stick to the knife. To make this job a little easier, I use a pair of clean kitchen scissors to cut the gumdrops in half. Not only does it save time, it saves sanity!

Spice Drops

The black pepper in this recipe doesn't add heat; it wonderfully boosts the other spices. Not only do these cookies taste like the holidays, they seem to get better with age! After a few days, they harden a bit, but dunked into coffee or tea, they're perfect!

DRY INGREDIENTS

1 cup white rice flour

1/2 cup sweet rice flour

1/4 cup potato starch

1 teaspoon baking powder

1 teaspoon ground cinnamon

1/2 teaspoon salt

1/2 teaspoon ground black pepper

1/4 teaspoon xanthan gum

1/4 teaspoon ground nutmeg

1/4 teaspoon ground cloves

WET INGREDIENTS

1/2 cup (1 stick) butter, softened

3/4 cup packed dark brown sugar

2 large eggs

1 teaspoon vanilla extract

1/2 teaspoon lemon extract

1/2 teaspoon anise extract

Dear Elizabeth,

These cookies have such a different but delicious taste! Every year I used to make a double batch for Christmas. After offering a cookie to guests, I would ask if they could guess my secret ingredient. No one ever guessed! (It's black pepper.) I would certainly love to bake these again. Would you consider creating a gluten-free version of this old family recipe? Thanks!

Stephanie M.
Wisconsin

1. In a medium bowl, whisk together dry ingredients.

2. In another medium bowl, cream together butter and brown sugar, about 1 minute. (Use medium-high on a handheld mixer, medium speed on a stand mixer.) Add eggs, 1 at a time, beating well after each addition. Add extracts and blend, 15 seconds. Reduce mixer speed to low and add dry ingredients. Mix until a dough forms.

3. Cover bowl with plastic wrap and refrigerate dough 2 hours or overnight.

4. Preheat oven to 350°F. Line 2 cookie sheets with parchment paper.

5. Drop dough by the teaspoonful onto prepared cookie sheets, placing cookies 2 inches apart.

6. Bake first sheet of cookies for 8 to 10 minutes or until cookies are golden brown and aromatic.

7. Remove cookie sheet from the oven and transfer cookies directly onto racks to cool completely. (These cookies love to stick to parchment paper. As soon as they come out of the oven, remove them from the pan. I use a sturdy metal cookie spatula. It is perfect for cookies like these that love to stick!) While first sheet cools, bake the second sheet of cookies.

Makes 4 to 5 dozen small cookies

Santa's Whiskers

A reader asked me to convert her favorite Christmas cookie recipe, Santa's Whiskers. This egg-free recipe is studded with candied cherries and pressed into coconut.

DRY INGREDIENTS
1 1/2 cups white rice flour
1/2 cup cornstarch
1/2 cup sweet rice flour
1/2 teaspoon xanthan gum

WET INGREDIENTS
1 cup (2 sticks) butter, softened
1 cup granulated sugar
2 tablespoons milk, plus more as needed
1 teaspoon vanilla extract
3/4 cup chopped candied cherries

2 cups flaked sweetened coconut

1. In a small bowl, whisk together dry ingredients.

2. In a large bowl, cream together butter and granulated sugar until light and fluffy. (Use high speed on a handheld mixer or medium-high on a stand mixer.) Add dry ingredients, milk, and vanilla; mix until dough forms. If dough is dry, add an additional tablespoon milk. Reduce mixer speed to medium-low. Add candied cherries.

3. Place flaked coconut in a dish. Roll dough by the tablespoonful into balls. Roll dough balls in coconut.

4. Place rolled cookies on a baking sheet and cover with plastic wrap. Chill dough balls overnight.

5. Preheat oven to 375°F. Line 2 cookie sheets with parchment paper.

6. Place cookies on prepared baking sheets about 2 inches apart. Bake first sheet for 10 to 12 minutes or until golden brown.

7. Remove cookie sheet from oven and place on wire racks to cool, 3 to 5 minutes. Transfer cookies directly onto racks to cool completely. While the first sheet cools, bake the second sheet of cookies.

Makes about 4 1/2 dozen cookies

Gimme a Kiss
Cookies

You know these cookies. A yummy peanut butter cookie with a Hershey's Kiss pressed into the middle. They are a holiday classic, although there's no reason why you can't make them all year long.

DRY INGREDIENTS

3/4 cup white rice flour

1/4 cup brown rice flour

1/4 cup sweet rice flour

1/2 teaspoon baking soda

1/2 teaspoon baking powder

WET INGREDIENTS

1/4 cup (1/2 stick) butter, softened

1/2 cup creamy peanut butter

3/4 cup packed dark brown sugar

1 large egg

1 teaspoon vanilla extract

1 (8-ounce) bag Hershey's Kisses (more if you plan to munch)

1/2 cup granulated sugar

1. Preheat oven to 350°F. Line 2 baking sheets with parchment paper.

2. In a small bowl, whisk together dry ingredients.

3. In a large bowl, cream butter, peanut butter, and brown sugar together until light and fluffy. (Use medium speed on handheld and stand mixers.) Add egg and vanilla; blend until thoroughly incorporated. Add dry ingredients; blend until thoroughly combined.

4. Place granulated sugar in a shallow dish. Roll cookie dough into tablespoon-size balls. Roll balls in sugar until coated. Place on 2 inches apart on cookie sheets. Press an unwrapped Hershey's Kiss into each cookie.

5. Bake first sheet of cookies for 10 to 12 minutes or until lightly brown.

6. Remove cookie sheet from oven and place on wire racks to cool, 3 to 5 minutes. Transfer cookies directly onto racks to cool completely. While first sheet is cooling, bake second sheet of cookies.

Makes about 3 dozen cookies

Candy Cane Cookies

DRY INGREDIENTS

2 cups white rice flour

1/2 cup sweet rice flour

1/4 cup cornstarch

1/4 teaspoon salt

1/4 teaspoon xanthan gum

WET INGREDIENTS

1 1/2 cups confectioners' sugar

1 cup (2 sticks) butter, softened

1 large egg

1 teaspoon peppermint extract

1 teaspoon vanilla extract

1/3 cup finely crushed candy canes

1/2 teaspoon red food color

Dear Elizabeth

I don't know where this recipe came from or how the tradition started, but the women in my family always make a huge batch of these cookies. The cookies have broken-up bits of candy cane in them. This adds a nice crunch and flavor to the cookie. Do you think they could be made gluten free?

Sandra L.
Connecticut

1. Preheat oven to 350°F. Line 2 cookie sheets with parchment paper.

2. In a medium bowl, whisk together dry ingredients.

3. In a large bowl, combine wet ingredients. Beat until light and creamy, about 45 seconds. (Use medium speed on a handheld mixer, medium-low on a stand mixer.) Reduce mixer speed to low; add dry ingredients and blend until thoroughly combined.

4. Divide dough in half. Stir crushed candy canes into half of the dough. Mix the food coloring into the remaining half of the dough. If you live in a warm climate, you might want to refrigerate your dough for 1 hour before shaping and baking.

5. To make the candy cane shape: Roll about 2 teaspoons of each dough into 4-inch ropes. Place the ropes side by side and gently twist and roll the dough together. Continue with the rest of the dough, making 1 cookie at a time.

6. Place cookies on prepared cookie sheets. Gently curve one end to form the "handle" of each cane.

7. Bake first sheet of cookies for 10 to 12 minutes or until lightly golden brown.

8. Remove cookie sheet from the oven and place on wire racks to cool, 2 minutes. Transfer cookies directly onto racks to cool completely. While first sheet is cooling, bake second sheet of cookies.

Makes about 5 dozen cookies

Eggnog Cookies

DRY INGREDIENTS

1 3/4 cups white rice flour, plus more for dusting

1/2 cup potato starch

1/4 cup cornstarch

1 teaspoon baking powder

1/2 teaspoon ground nutmeg

1/4 teaspoon salt

1/4 teaspoon xanthan gum

WET INGREDIENTS

1/2 cup (1 stick) butter, softened

3/4 cup granulated sugar

1/3 cup eggnog

1 large egg

1 teaspoon vanilla extract

Eggnog Icing (see recipe, facing page)

Dear Elizabeth,

The year before my diagnosis, I made these wonderful eggnog cookies. They were a hit. I'd love to make the recipe again, and I am sure your readers would be delighted with the taste of these cookies. They really taste like eggnog!

Emily S.
New York

1. In a medium bowl, whisk together dry ingredients.

2. In a large bowl, cream butter and sugar together until light and fluffy, about 45 seconds. (Use medium-high speed with a handheld mixer, medium speed with a stand mixer.) Reduce mixer speed to low and add eggnog, egg, and vanilla; beat for 15 seconds. Increase mixer speed (high for a handheld mixer, medium-high for stand mixer) and beat for 1 minute. Add dry ingredients and mix for 30 seconds or until well combined.

3. Divide dough in half. Pat each half into a disk and wrap tightly in plastic wrap. Refrigerate 2 hours or overnight.

4. Preheat oven to 350°F. Line 2 cookie sheets with parchment paper.

5. Dust a work surface lightly with rice flour. Roll out dough to about 1/4 inch thick. Cut dough with your favorite cookie cutters (dip cookie cutter in rice flour before using to prevent dough from sticking to cutter), placing cookies onto prepared cookie sheets.

6. Bake first sheet of cookies for 8 to 10 minutes or until edges are lightly browned. (Time will vary greatly depending on the size of your cookies. I used 3-inch cutters and the cookies took about 9 minutes to bake.)

7. Remove cookie sheet from the oven and place on wire racks to cool, 3 to 5 minutes. Transfer cookies directly onto racks to cool completely. While first sheet is cooling, bake the second sheet of cookies.

8. Ice cooled cookies.

Yield will vary depending on the size cutters used; makes about 2 dozen 3-inch cookies.

Eggnog Icing

1/4 cup eggnog
3 cups confectioners' sugar
Food coloring (optional)

1. Combine eggnog and confectioners' sugar. Stir until smooth.

2. If desired, divide and place into small mixing bowls, depending on how many colors you want to use. Add a few drops of food coloring to each and stir to combine.

Pecan Tassies

DRY INGREDIENTS
1/2 cup white rice flour
1/4 cup sweet rice flour
1/4 cup cornstarch
1/4 teaspoon xanthan gum

WET INGREDIENTS
4 ounces cream cheese, softened
1/2 cup (1 stick) butter, softened

Filling
1 large egg
3/4 cup packed dark brown sugar
1 teaspoon vanilla extract
3/4 cup finely chopped pecans

Dear Elizabeth,

I've got a request for you! Pecan Tassies! Every Christmas my mom makes a batch of these cookie-tarts. On Christmas Eve, the adults in our family exchange gifts. A strong cup of coffee and more than a few of these goodies make the evening even more special. Hope you can help.

Debbie B.
Washington

1. In a medium bowl, whisk together dry ingredients.

2. In another medium bowl, mix cream cheese and butter until light and creamy. (Use medium-high speed with a handheld mixer, medium speed with a stand mixer.) Add dry ingredients. Blend until combined. Cover and refrigerate for 1 hour.

3. Meanwhile, prepare filling. In a small bowl, beat egg lightly. Add brown sugar and vanilla; mix well. Add pecans and stir until evenly coated.

4. Preheat oven to 375°F. Divide and shape dough into 24 balls.

5. Place 1 ball of dough in each of 24 miniature muffin pan cups or mini tart pans. Press dough onto bottoms and up sides of cups to form shells.

6. Spoon filling evenly into pastry shells, filling each shell about three quarters full.

7. Bake Tassies for 25 to 30 minutes or until lightly browned.

8. Remove pans from oven and set on wire racks to cool, for 5 minutes. Remove Tassies from pan and place directly onto racks to cool completely.

Makes 2 dozen Pecan Tassies

Snowballs/Mexican Wedding Cookies

Eleven months out of the year, I call these Mexican Wedding cookies. However, during December, I make batches of them, pack them into cellophane bags, and affix a tag that reads "Snowballs." With their thick coating of confectioners' sugar that's just what they look like.

DRY INGREDIENTS

1 1/4 cups white rice flour
1/2 cup sweet rice flour
1/4 cup cornstarch
1/2 teaspoon xanthan gum

WET INGREDIENTS

1 cup (2 sticks) butter, softened
1/2 cup plus 1 pound confectioners' sugar
2 teaspoons vanilla extract

1. Preheat oven to 350°F. Line 2 baking sheets with parchment paper.

2. In a small bowl, whisk together dry ingredients.

3. In a medium bowl, cream together butter and 1/2 cup confectioners' sugar until light and fluffy. (Use medium speed on both handheld and stand mixers.) Add dry ingredients and vanilla; mix for 1 minute.

4. Roll cookie dough into tablespoon-size balls. Place 2 inches apart on prepared cookie sheets.

5. Bake first sheet of cookies for 15 minutes or until lightly golden brown.

6. Meanwhile, fill a 9x13-inch pan with 1 pound confectioners' sugar.

7. Remove cookie sheet from the oven. Immediately place cookies in confectioners' sugar. Bury cookies so all surfaces are covered. Once first sheet of cookies is in confectioners' sugar, bake second sheet of cookies. Allow cookies to sit in sugar overnight.

8. Remove cookies from confectioners' sugar, shaking off excess sugar.

Makes about 2 dozen cookies

Chocolate
Pixies

Part brownie, part cookie, these Chocolate Pixies taste as good as they look!

DRY INGREDIENTS

1 1/2 cups white rice flour

1/2 cup cornstarch

2 tablespoons sweet rice flour

1/4 teaspoon xanthan gum

2 teaspoons baking powder

1/2 teaspoon salt

WET INGREDIENTS

1/4 cup (1/2 stick) butter, melted (see Baker's Note)

4 squares (4 ounces) unsweetened chocolate

2 cups granulated sugar

4 large eggs

1/2 cup chopped walnuts (optional)

Confectioners' sugar, for rolling

Dear Elizabeth,

Every Sunday in the 1950s we visited my grand-parents, who owned a dairy farm in Ellicottville, New York. Grandma's cookie jar was always inviting and full of chocolate delicacies. Now that celiac disease has been identified in several family members, we would appreciate it if you could make the following recipe gluten free.

Mary B.
New York

1. In a medium bowl, whisk together dry ingredients.

2. In a microwave safe bowl, melt chocolate. (Microwave chocolate for 20 seconds, then remove the bowl from the microwave and stir. Repeat until completely melted.) In a large bowl, combine melted chocolate and melted butter, stirring well, about 30 seconds. Add sugar; blend on medium speed, 45 seconds. Add eggs; mix on medium speed, 30 seconds. Scrape down the sides of the bowl. Add dry ingredients; mix on medium speed, 45 seconds. Add nuts, if using, and stir to combine. The dough will look like thick brownie batter.

3. Cover dough with plastic wrap and chill in the refrigerator for 4 hours or overnight.

4. Preheat oven to 350°F. Line 2 baking sheets with parchment paper.

5. Roll dough into balls about 1 tablespoon each.

6. Place confectioners' sugar in a shallow dish and roll dough balls in sugar. Place dough balls on prepared baking sheets, placing about 3 inches apart. Return one sheet of cookies to the refrigerator while the first sheet bakes. It is important to keep dough chilled.

7. Bake first sheet of cookies for 10 to 12 minutes or until cookies have a cracked appearance and are very aromatic.

8. Remove cookie sheet from oven and place on wire racks to cool, 3 to 5 minutes. Transfer cookies directly onto racks to cool completely. While first sheet is cooling, bake second sheet of cookies.

Makes 4 dozen cookies

Baker's Note

Butter and chocolate melt at two different temperatures, so it's easier to melt them separately. I always melt my butter and chocolate in the microwave. By melting them separately, I am guaranteed the butter won't spurt all over the microwave while the chocolate finishes melting.

Molasses Crackle Cookies

DRY INGREDIENTS

1 1/2 cups white rice flour, plus more for
    dusting hands
1/2 cup cornstarch
1 tablespoon ground ginger
2 teaspoons baking soda
1 teaspoon ground cinnamon
1/2 teaspoon xanthan gum
1/2 teaspoon salt

WET INGREDIENTS

1 cup granulated sugar, plus more for rolling
3/4 cup vegetable shortening
1/4 cup unsulphured molasses
1 large egg

Dear Elizabeth

During the holidays, these cookies were the only cookies I baked. They are a family tradition. I liked how easy they were to make and how pretty they turned out. Since going on a gluten-free diet, I have missed making them. If you could make the recipe gluten free, I'd be thrilled.

Cynthia K.
Pennsylvania

1. Preheat oven to 350°F. Line 2 baking sheets with parchment paper.

2. In a medium bowl, whisk together dry ingredients.

3. In a large bowl, cream sugar and vegetable shortening together on medium-high speed with both handheld and stand mixers, about 45 seconds. Add the molasses and egg; mix on medium-high speed, 30 seconds. Add the dry ingredients. Blend on medium speed, 1 minute.

4. Place some sugar in a shallow dish. Dust your hands with white rice flour. Roll dough into tablespoon-size balls. Roll the dough balls into the sugar. Place balls on prepared cookie sheets, about 2 inches apart.

5. Bake first sheet of cookies for 12 minutes or until the cookies are brown and aromatic.

6. Remove cookie sheets from the oven and place on wire racks to cool, 3 to 5 minutes. Transfer cookies directly onto racks to cool completely. While first sheet cools, bake second sheet of cookies.

Makes 3 dozen cookies

Baker's Note

The best way to measure molasses, or anything sticky, is to first spray a thin coat of cooking spray into the measuring cup or pour a little cooking oil onto a paper towel and wipe the inside of the measuring cup.

No-Bake
Peanut Butter Balls

This easy recipe is a holiday classic in my home. I think they taste like Reese's Peanut Butter Cups—only better.

1 cup plus 1 tablespoon creamy peanut butter
   (do not use "natural" peanut butter)
3 tablespoons butter, melted
2 cups confectioners' sugar
8 ounces dark chocolate

1. Line a cookie sheet with parchment paper.

2. Combine all ingredients except chocolate in a large bowl. Blend until smooth, about 45 seconds on medium speed for both handheld and stand mixers.

3. Cover dough with plastic wrap and chill, 2 hours.

4. Roll dough into 1-tablespoon-size balls.

5. Melt chocolate in a microwave-safe bowl. (Microwave chocolate for 20 seconds, then remove the bowl from the microwave and stir. Repeat until completely melted.)

6. Dip cookies into melted chocolate. Place dipped cookies onto a parchment lined baking sheet. Allow to harden in the refrigerator for 1 hour or until chocolate is set.

7. Remove cookies from the refrigerator and store in an airtight container.

Makes 2 dozen cookies

Brownies and Bar Cookies

Brownies

If you have ever attended a gluten-free gathering you know that pans and pans of brownies always appear on the table. This recipe is so easy to make that you too can bring a pan of brownies to your next celiac gathering.

Gluten-free nonstick cooking spray

DRY INGREDIENTS
1 cup white rice flour
1/2 cup cornstarch
1/2 cup cocoa powder
1/2 teaspoon salt
1/4 teaspoon xanthan gum

WET INGREDIENTS
1 cup (2 sticks) butter, softened
2 cups granulated sugar
4 large eggs
2 teaspoons vanilla extract

1. Preheat oven to 325°F. Grease a 9x13-inch baking pan with cooking spray.

2. In a medium bowl, whisk together dry ingredients.

3. In a large bowl, cream together butter and sugar. (Use medium-high speed with a handheld mixer or medium speed with a stand mixer.) Add eggs; mix until combined. Reduce mixer speed to medium for handheld mixer and medium-low for stand mixer. Add dry ingredients and vanilla; mix until a batter forms.

4. Spread batter into prepared pan. Bake for 35 to 40 minutes.

5. Remove pan from the oven and place on a wire rack to cool completely. Cut into 12 squares.

Makes 1 dozen brownies

Mint Brownies

Gluten-free nonstick cooking spray

WET INGREDIENTS

1 cup granulated sugar

1/4 teaspoon salt

2 large eggs

2 squares (2 ounces) unsweetened chocolate

1/2 cup (1 stick) butter, melted

1/8 teaspoon pure peppermint oil, or to taste
   (see note)

DRY INGREDIENTS

1/2 cup white rice flour

1/4 cup cornstarch

For the Icing

1 cup confectioners' sugar

1/4 cup (1/2 stick) butter, softened

2 tablespoons milk

Green food coloring (optional)

3 candy canes, crushed (optional)

Dear Elizabeth

I love everything mint. These brownies were my favorite holiday recipe. I have tried several times to convert the recipe, but I have not had any luck. I am sure you will have better luck than I did!

Veronica G.
Colorado

1. Preheat oven to 350°F. Lightly grease a 9x9-inch pan with cooking spray.

2. In a medium bowl, beat together the sugar, salt, and eggs for 30 seconds. (You can do this by hand; you don't need an electric mixer.) Melt the chocolate. (In a microwave-safe bowl, melt chocolate for 20 seconds, then remove the bowl from the microwave and stir. Repeat until completely melted.) Add melted chocolate and melted butter to the egg mixture; stir to combine, about 15 seconds. Add white rice flour, cornstarch, and peppermint oil; mix for 45 seconds.

3. Pour the batter into prepared pan. Bake for 25 minutes or until a tester inserted into the center of the pan comes out clean.

4. Place the pan on a wire rack to cool completely.

5. Meanwhile, make the icing: In a small bowl, combine the confectioners' sugar, butter, and milk; mix on medium speed for 1 minute. Add food coloring, if desired, and combine thoroughly.

6. Spread the icing over the cooled brownies. Sprinkle the crushed candy canes over the brownies, if using. Cut into 12 squares.

Makes 1 dozen brownies

Ingredient Note
Pure peppermint oil is very, very strong. If you can't find it, you can use peppermint extract. Add 1/2 teaspoon peppermint extract. Smell the batter. If you can detect peppermint, you have added enough. If you can't, add a little more extract.

Cheesecake Brownies

This recipe is perfect for Valentine's Day. Get out a heart cookie cutter and, once the brownies have cooled, cut these into heart shapes.

Gluten-free nonstick cooking spray

DRY INGREDIENTS
1/2 cup white rice flour
1/4 cup cornstarch
2 tablespoons potato starch
1/2 teaspoon xanthan gum

WET INGREDIENTS
31/2 ounces unsweetened chocolate
1/2 cup (1 stick) butter, melted
11/4 cups granulated sugar
3 large eggs

Cheesecake Layer
1 (8-ounce) package cream cheese, softened
1 large egg
1/3 cup granulated sugar
2 teaspoons white rice flour
1/2 teaspoon vanilla extract

1. Preheat oven to 350°F. Grease an 8-inch square pan with cooking spray.

2. In a small bowl, whisk together dry ingredients.

3. Melt chocolate. (Microwave chocolate for 20 seconds, then remove the bowl from the microwave and stir. Repeat until completely melted.) In a medium bowl, combine melted chocolate and melted butter. Stir to combine. Stir in sugar; mixture will be thick. Add the eggs, 1 at a time, to the sugar-chocolate mixture. Blend on low speed with handheld or stand mixer after each addition. Once the eggs are added, blend until smooth. Add the dry ingredients and blend for 1 minute on medium speed.

4. Spread the batter evenly into the prepared pan. Batter will be thick.

5. Prepare the cheesecake layer: In a medium bowl, beat together the cream cheese, egg, sugar, white rice flour, and vanilla; mix on medium speed for 1 minute or until smooth. Gently spread the cheesecake batter on top of the brownie batter. Using a butter knife, swirl the two layers together to make a marbled top.

6. Bake for 40 to 45 minutes or until a tester inserted into the center comes out clean.

7. Remove pan from the oven and place on a wire rack to cool completely, then chill in the refrigerator for 2 hours before cutting into 12 squares.

8. Store any leftover cheesecake brownies in the refrigerator.

Makes 1 dozen brownies

Baker's Note
When these brownies come out of the oven, they will be puffy. Upon cooling, they will fall slightly. Don't panic. This is supposed to happen.

Brown Sugar Butter Bars

This is by far the easiest recipe I have made in a long time. A quick scan of the ingredients reveals there isn't anything out of the ordinary: just dry ingredients, brown sugar, butter, and an egg. There isn't even vanilla! The butter and brown sugar are cooked on the stove, which coaxes out nuanced flavors in both—think deep caramel and brown butter!

Gluten-free nonstick cooking spray

WET INGREDIENTS

1/2 cup (1 stick) butter, softened
1 cup packed dark brown sugar
1 large egg

DRY INGREDIENTS

3/4 cup white rice flour
1/4 cup cornstarch
1/4 cup sweet rice flour
1 teaspoon baking soda
1/2 teaspoon xanthan gum

1. Preheat oven to 350°F. Grease an 8-inch square baking pan with cooking spray.

2. In a small saucepan, combine butter and brown sugar. Melt over medium heat, stirring occasionally.

3. Meanwhile, whisk together dry ingredients in a medium bowl.

4. Once butter mixture is melted and smooth, remove from heat. Allow to cool for 1 minute. Stir in dry ingredients and egg (you can use a wooden spoon); mix until thoroughly combined.

5. Spread mixture evenly into prepared pan with a spatula (the batter is a little thick). Don't worry about not having enough batter. Even though it looks like there isn't enough, there is! Bake for 20 to 25 minutes or until a tester inserted into the center of the bars comes out clean.

6. Remove pan from oven and place on a wire rack to cool completely. Cut into 16 squares.

Makes 16 bars

Chocolate Chip Cookie Cake

In the eighth grade, I was lucky to be in Mrs. Staph's homeroom. Not only was she an excellent teacher, she was also an outstanding baker. To celebrate students' birthdays, Mrs. Staph always made a chocolate chip cookie cake. Everyone loved these cakes. Now you can enjoy them too!

Gluten-free nonstick cooking spray

DRY INGREDIENTS
1 1/4 cups white rice flour
1/2 cup sweet rice flour
1/4 cup cornstarch
1 teaspoon baking soda
1/2 teaspoon salt

WET INGREDIENTS
3/4 cup (1 1/2 sticks) butter, softened
1/4 cup granulated sugar
1 cup packed dark brown sugar
2 teaspoons vanilla extract
3 large eggs
1 (12-ounce) bag semi-sweet chocolate chips

1. Preheat oven to 350°F. Grease a 9x13-inch baking pan with cooking spray.

2. In a medium bowl, whisk together dry ingredients.

3. In a large bowl, cream butter, sugars, and vanilla together until blended, 30 to 45 seconds. (Use medium-high speed on handheld and stand mixers.) The butter will look like a grainy paste. Add eggs, 1 at a time, mixing well between each addition. Add dry ingredients and blend until a dough forms. (Use medium speed on a handheld mixer; medium-low on a stand mixer.) Using a wooden spoon, stir in chocolate chips.

4. Spread dough evenly into prepared pan. Bake for 45 minutes or until a tester inserted into the center of the cake comes out clean.

5. Remove pan from oven and place on a wire rack to cool. Cut into 12 squares.

Makes 1 dozen bars

Lemon Bars

Tart lemon filling atop a buttery shortbread crust makes these the best lemon bars I have tasted. With a light yellow color, they are perfect for spring.

Gluten-free nonstick cooking spray

DRY INGREDIENTS
1/4 cup sweet rice flour
1/2 cup white rice flour
1/4 cup cornstarch
1/2 teaspoon xanthan gum
1/4 cup confectioners' sugar

WET INGREDIENTS
1/2 cup (1 stick) cold butter, cut into small pieces
2 tablespoons water

Topping
2 large eggs
3/4 cup granulated sugar
2 tablespoons white rice flour
1/4 cup freshly squeezed lemon juice

1. Preheat oven to 350°F. Grease an 8-inch square pan with cooking spray.

2. Place the dry ingredients in a food processor and pulse once or twice to combine. Add butter; pulse mixture until butter is thoroughly incorporated. (Dough should resemble a coarse meal.) Add water; pulse a few times until a dough forms.

3. Press mixture into the bottom of the prepared pan. Bake crust for 35 to 40 minutes or until golden brown.

4. Remove pan from oven, leaving oven on. Place pan on a wire rack to cool.

5. Make the topping: In a small bowl, combine eggs, granulated sugar, white rice flour, and lemon juice. Pour mixture over baked crust.

6. Return pan to oven. Bake for 15 minutes or until filling is set. (Filling should be firm and not jiggle.)

7. Remove pan from oven and place on a wire rack to cool. Cut into 12 squares.

Makes 1 dozen bars

Gooey Butter Bars

These bars are amazing served warm! Gooey and buttery, as the name implies, these bars melt in your mouth.

Gluten-free nonstick cooking spray

DRY INGREDIENTS
1/2 cup white rice flour
1/4 cup sweet rice flour
1/4 cup potato starch
1/2 teaspoon salt
1/4 teaspoon baking soda
1/4 teaspoon xanthan gum

WET INGREDIENTS
1/2 cup (1 stick) butter, softened
1/2 cup granulated sugar
1 large egg
1 teaspoon vanilla extract

Filling
1 (8-ounce) package cream cheese, softened
4 cups confectioners' sugar
2 large eggs
1/4 cup (1/2 stick) butter, melted
1 teaspoon pure vanilla extract

Dear Elizabeth,

I used to make a recipe called Gooey Butter Bars. They are a ridiculously rich cake/blond brownie that my family adores. The thing is, my recipe used cake mix. I've tried gluten-free cake mixes, but they just don't come out right. Can you adapt the recipe for me? Thanks!

Linda R.
Georgia

1. Preheat oven to 350°F. Lightly grease a 9x9-inch square baking pan with cooking spray.

2. In a small bowl, whisk together dry ingredients.

3. In a medium bowl, cream together the butter and sugar until a thick paste forms. (Use high speed on a handheld mixer, medium-high on a stand mixer.) Add the egg and vanilla; mix until smooth and thoroughly combined. Add the dry ingredients and mix until a batter forms.

4. Spread the dough evenly into prepared pan.

5. Make the filling: In another medium bowl, cream together the cream cheese and confectioners' sugar. (Use medium-high on handheld and stand mixers.) Add the eggs, melted butter, and vanilla. Beat for 15 seconds.

6. Spread the filling evenly over the base. Bake for 30 to 35 minutes or until the filling is just set; you want the filling to still be gooey.

7. Remove pan from the oven and set on a wire rack to cool completely.

8. Cover bars with plastic wrap and refrigerate overnight or serve warm. Cut into 24 squares.

Makes 2 dozen small bars

Blondies

I always read that blondies are "blond brownies." To me, brownies are defined by their chocolate. I think blondies are best described as rich, butterscotchy bar cookies. Don't let the description "butterscotch" scare you. These are not cloyingly sweet.

Gluten-free nonstick cooking spray

DRY INGREDIENTS
3/4 cup white rice flour
1/4 cup sweet rice flour
1/4 cup cornstarch
1 1/2 teaspoons baking powder
1/2 teaspoon salt

WET INGREDIENTS
1/2 cup (1 stick) butter, softened
1 cup packed dark brown sugar
2 large eggs
1/2 teaspoon butterscotch oil or 2 teaspoons
   vanilla extract

1. Preheat oven to 350°F. Grease an 8-inch square pan with cooking spray.

2. In a small bowl, whisk together dry ingredients.

3. In a medium bowl, cream together butter and brown sugar until light and fluffy. (Use medium-high speed on handheld mixer, medium speed on stand mixer.) Add eggs, 1 at a time, mixing well after each addition. Add dry ingredients and butterscotch oil or vanilla. Blend for 1 minute. Batter will be thick.

4. Pour batter into prepared pan. Bake for 35 to 45 minutes or until a tester inserted into the center of the pan comes out clean.

5. Remove pan from oven and place on a wire rack to cool completely. Cut into 12 squares.

Makes 1 dozen bars

Baker's Note
1 cup of chocolate chips and/or 1/2 cup chopped nuts make nice additions to this recipe. Fold them in after adding the flavoring.

Quick Carrot Cake Bars

Gluten-free nonstick cooking spray

DRY INGREDIENTS

1 1/4 cups white rice flour

1/4 cup sweet rice flour

1/4 cup cornstarch

2/3 cup granulated sugar

2 teaspoons baking soda

1 1/2 teaspoons ground cinnamon

1/2 teaspoon ground nutmeg

1/2 teaspoon salt

WET INGREDIENTS

3/4 cup unsweetened applesauce

1/4 cup vegetable oil

3 large eggs

3 cups finely grated carrots

Confectioners' sugar, for dusting (optional)

Cream cheese icing (optional)
   (see recipe, facing page)

Dear Elizabeth,

I love carrot cake. Since having a big cake around isn't always feasible, I created this recipe years ago. Over the years, I lightened up the recipe with applesauce. It's excellent, moist, and flavorful. Occasionally, when I feel like a splurge, I'll ice the bars with cream cheese icing. Last fall I was diagnosed a celiac. Lately I've been craving these bars. Please consider converting the recipe.

Eliza G.
Arizona

1. Preheat oven to 350°F. Lightly grease a 9x13-inch pan with cooking spray.

2. In a large bowl, whisk together dry ingredients.

3. In a small bowl, combine the applesauce, oil, and eggs. Pour mixture over the dry ingredients and mix until a batter forms. (Use medium speed on handheld and stand mixers.) Add the carrots and stir until combined.

4. Pour the batter evenly into the prepared pan. Bake the cake for about 1 hour and 10 minutes or until a tester inserted in the middle of the cake comes out clean. (Some damp crumbs might cling, but you shouldn't see any wet batter.)

5. Remove the pan from the oven and place on a wire rack to cool completely.

6. Cut into 12 squares. Dust with confectioners' sugar or ice with cream cheese icing, if desired.

Makes 1 dozen bars

Easy Cream Cheese Icing

1 (4-ounce) package cream cheese, softened
2 tablespoons butter, softened
2 teaspoons vanilla extract
2 cups confectioners' sugar

1. Cream together cream cheese and butter until light and fluffy. (Use medium-high speed on handheld and stand mixers.) Add vanilla and confectioners' sugar and mix until smooth. If icing is too thick for your taste, add a few teaspoons of milk.

Honey
Bars

When developing these bars, I knew they needed something. I just couldn't put my finger on what, exactly. I tried molasses, golden syrup and brown corn syrup. Nothing tasted right. Then, it hit me. Honey! After one bite, I knew the recipe was complete.

Gluten-free nonstick cooking spray

DRY INGREDIENTS

1 cup white rice flour

1/4 cup potato starch

1/4 cup cornstarch

1 teaspoon baking powder

1/2 teaspoon salt

1/4 teaspoon xanthan gum

WET INGREDIENTS

1/2 cup solid vegetable shortening (do not use butter)

1/2 cup packed dark brown sugar

1/2 cup honey

1 large egg

1 teaspoon vanilla extract

1. Preheat oven to 350°F. Grease an 8-inch square baking pan with cooking spray.

2. In a medium bowl, whisk together dry ingredients.

3. In a large bowl, combine wet ingredients. Blend for about 30 seconds. (Use high speed on a handheld mixer, medium-high on a stand mixer.) Add dry ingredients; blend for 45 seconds.

4. Spread batter into prepared pan. Bake for 25 to 30 minutes, or until a tester inserted into the middle comes out clean.

5. Remove pan from oven and place on a wire rack to cool completely. Cut into 9 or 12 squares.

Makes 9 to 12 bars

Banana Bars

This recipe is a cross between a banana muffin and a banana cake. It is pleasantly sweet with lovely banana and vanilla flavors.

Gluten-free nonstick cooking spray

DRY INGREDIENTS
1 1/4 cups white rice flour
1/4 cup potato starch
1/2 cup cornstarch
2 teaspoons baking powder
1/2 teaspoon xanthan gum
1/2 teaspoon salt

WET INGREDIENTS
1/4 cup vegetable shortening
1 cup granulated sugar
2 large eggs
1 cup mashed ripe bananas (2 to 3 large bananas)
1 1/2 teaspoons vanilla extract

1. Preheat oven to 350°F. Grease a 9x13-inch pan with cooking spray.

2. In a medium bowl, whisk together dry ingredients.

3. In a large bowl, combine wet ingredients. Blend until thoroughly combined. (Use medium-high speed on a handheld mixer, medium speed on a stand mixer.) Add dry ingredients and blend until smooth.

4. Spread batter evenly into prepared pan. Bake 20 to 25 minutes or until a tester inserted into the center of the cake comes out clean.

5. Remove pan from the oven and place on a wire rack to cool completely. Cut into 9 or 12 squares.

Makes 9 to 12 bars

Blueberry
Cheesecake Bars

In addition to blueberries, try this recipe with raspberries and raspberry jam or strawberries and strawberry jam. Honestly, any summer fruit would be outstanding!

For the Crust
6 tablespoons butter, melted
2 cups gluten-free graham cracker crumbs

For the Filling
2 (8-ounce) packages cream cheese, softened
3/4 cup granulated sugar
2 large eggs
2 teaspoons vanilla extract
1 (10-ounce) jar blueberry jam or preserves
1 cup fresh blueberries, washed and picked over

Dear Elizabeth,

Thanks so much for all your recipes. I wanted to share a recipe with your readers for a cheesecake I've been making for years. When I was diagnosed, it was easy to convert this recipe to gluten free. I just needed to use gluten-free cookies instead of my traditional graham crackers. Honestly, I don't think anyone even noticed! Anytime I'm invited to a cookout, this cheesecake comes with me. I hope you enjoy it!

Laurel M.
Maine

1. Preheat oven to 350°F. Make the crust: In a small bowl, combine melted butter and graham cracker crumbs. Stir until thoroughly combined.

2. Press crumb mixture firmly onto the bottom of a 9x13-inch pan. Bake crust for 10 minutes or until light brown and aromatic.

3. Remove crust from the oven and place on a wire rack to cool. Leave oven on.

4. Make the filling: In a medium bowl, beat cream cheese until light and creamy. (Use medium-high speed on a handheld mixer, medium speed on a stand mixer.) Add sugar, eggs, and vanilla; beat until well blended.

5. Spread jam evenly over baked crust. Sprinkle blueberries evenly over the jam. Using a knife or spatula, spread cream cheese mixture over the blueberries. (It's not a big deal if the blueberries roll around.)

6. Return pan to the oven to cook, 30 to 35 minutes or until filling no longer jiggles.

7. Remove the pan from the oven and place on a wire rack to cool completely. Cut into 12 or 15 bars. Store any leftover bars in the refrigerator up to 3 days.

Makes 12 to 15 bars

Baker's Note

This recipe requires spreading the blueberry jam over the graham cracker crumbs, which can be difficult. If you pour the jam evenly over the crust, you won't need to do much spreading at all. If the jam starts to pick up crumbs, don't worry; it doesn't really affect the finished product.

Maple
Brownies

I live in maple syrup country. Each spring, large buckets are attached to maple trees to catch the sap. To celebrate the wonderfully unique flavor of maple, I decided to create a maple brownie. It's a take on blondies. Sweet, but not cloying, I like these almost as much as I like chocolate brownies.

Gluten-free nonstick cooking spray

DRY INGREDIENTS

2/3 cup white rice flour

1/3 cup cornstarch

1/3 cup sweet rice flour

1/2 teaspoon salt

1/2 teaspoon baking soda

1/2 teaspoon xanthan gum

WET INGREDIENTS

1/2 cup (1 stick) butter, softened

1/4 cup granulated sugar

1/2 cup packed dark brown sugar

1 large egg

1/2 teaspoon vanilla extract

1/2 cup pure maple syrup, preferably Grade B

1. Preheat oven to 350°F. Grease a 9-inch square baking pan with cooking spray.

2. In a small bowl, whisk together dry ingredients.

3. In a medium bowl, cream together butter, granulated sugar, and brown sugar for 1 minute. (Use high speed on a handheld mixer, medium-high speed on a stand mixer.) Add egg and mix until thoroughly combined. Add half of the dry ingredients; blend until smooth, about 30 seconds. Add vanilla and maple syrup; mix until thoroughly combined. Add remaining dry ingredients and mix for 1 minute.

4. Spread batter evenly into prepared pan. Bake for 25 to 30 minutes or until golden brown.

5. Remove pan from oven and place on a wire rack to cool completely. Cut into 9 or 12 squares.

Makes 9 to 12 brownies

Baker's Note

For the best maple flavor use Grade B maple syrup. Grade B is sometimes called "cooking syrup." This syrup is made at the end of the maple season. It has a pronounced maple flavor and deep, rich color. I get my Grade B syrup from Dakin Farms. If you're not near Vermont, you can get it online at www.dakinfarm.com.

Pumpkin Cheesecake Bars

Easier to make than a cheesecake or pie, this dessert is perfect for Thanksgiving. The bars need to be refrigerated overnight, so be sure to make them at least a day before.

Crust

2 cups gluten-free gingersnap crumbs (Mi-Del gluten-free gingersnaps ground fine in a food processor)

3 tablespoons granulated sugar

6 tablespoons butter, melted

Topping

2 (8-ounce) packages cream cheese, softened

3/4 cup granulated sugar

2 large eggs

1 (16-ounce) can pure pumpkin

2 teaspoons ground cinnamon

1 1/2 teaspoons ground allspice

1/2 teaspoon ground ginger

1 1/2 teaspoons vanilla extract

1. Make the crust: Preheat oven to 375°F. In a small bowl, combine gingersnap crumbs, sugar, and butter. Stir together with a fork until all ingredients are combined.

2. Press crumb mixture into the bottom of a 9x13-inch baking pan. Bake for 10 minutes or until lightly golden brown.

3. Remove pan from oven and place on a wire rack to cool. Reduce oven temperature to 325°F.

4. Make the topping: In a large bowl, cream together cream cheese and sugar; mix on low speed for about 1 minute. Add eggs 1 at a time. Add pumpkin and spices. Blend on low speed for 1 minute.

5. Pour pumpkin mixture onto cooled crust and bake for 25 to 30 minutes or until filling is set and does not jiggle.

6. Remove pan from the oven and place on a wire rack to cool completely.

7. Cover pan and place in the refrigerator overnight.

8. Remove pan from the refrigerator and cut into 12 squares. Store, covered, in the refrigerator until ready to serve.

Makes 1 dozen bars

Cereal Bars

Gluten-free nonstick cooking spray

5 tablespoons butter, softened
7 cups mini marshmallows
4 1/2 cups Glutino Honey Nut Cereal
1 cup rice bran crackers, broken into small pieces
1/2 cup dried cranberries (or cherry-flavored Craisins)

Dear Elizabeth,

My daughter was just diagnosed with celiac and she misses the Cheerios cereal bars that she ate in the college cafeteria. I'd love a recipe. Can you help?

Michelle K.
Pennslyvania

1. Line a 9x13-inch pan with parchment paper. Allow parchment paper to hang over the edges by about 3 inches. (Or grease the pan generously with cooking spray.)

2. In a large pot, combine butter and mini marshmallows. Cook over medium-low heat, stirring frequently, until smooth.

3. Turn off heat. Add cereal, rice bran crackers, and dried cranberries. Use a wooden spoon to stir until thoroughly combined. (Be sure to get to the bottom of your pan. Sometimes the marshmallow mixture likes to stick to the bottom.)

4. Transfer mixture to the prepared pan. Quickly coat your hands with a gluten-free cooking spray. Pat the mixture firmly into the pan.

5. Cover and refrigerate for 2 to 3 hours or until cold. Remove bars from the pan by lifting up on the overhanging parchment paper. Cut into 8 bars.

Makes 8 bars

Cakes

Cakes celebrate life's milestones: birthdays, weddings, anniversaries—but anytime a cake is on the table, life feels special. Here are a few tips to ensure yours are perfect every time.

Preparing Your Pan(s)

To prevent your cake from sticking to the pan, generously grease it with a solid shortening and dust with white rice flour. For chocolate cakes, use cocoa powder to dust the pan. Or use a gluten-free nonstick cooking spray and generously spray all sides of the pan. For cupcakes, line your cupcake pan with paper liners.

Checking Cakes for Doneness

1. Look at the cake. Does it jiggle when you open the oven door? If it does, don't stick a tester into the center of the cake. It might collapse. The cake should not jiggle at all when you stick a tester into the center.

2. Insert a tester or long skewer into the center of the cake. Be sure to hit the bottom of the pan when you test your cake. When removed, the tester should be free of batter. A few baked crumbs might cling to the tester. That's fine; just be sure there's no raw batter.

3. When a cake comes out of the oven, touch the top. Does it feel firm and springy? To teach yourself to feel cakes, use a tester first, then touch the cake. Over time, you'll develop muscle memory for checking a cake.

Cooling a Cake

Allow the cake to cool in the pan for five minutes, then invert onto a wire rack to cool completely.

Icing

Icing a cake should be a fun experience, not a stress-filled one. Make sure your cake has cooled completely before you begin icing.

Freezing

Un-iced cakes and cupcakes freeze very well.

Orange Chocolate Chip Cake

Not only does this cake possess great flavor, it is one of those crossover goodies: It's perfect for breakfast, a snack, or a light dessert.

Vegetable shortening, for pan
White rice flour, for pan

DRY INGREDIENTS
2 cups white rice flour
1/2 cup tapioca starch
1/2 cup sweet rice flour
1 tablespoon baking powder
1 teaspoon xanthan gum

WET INGREDIENTS
3/4 cup (1 1/2 sticks) butter, softened
1 3/4 cups granulated sugar
4 large eggs
1 teaspoon vanilla extract
1 tablespoon grated orange zest
1 cup orange juice
1 1/2 cups chocolate chips (milk, dark, or white)

Confectioners' sugar, for dusting (optional)

1. Preheat oven to 350°F. Grease and rice flour a 12-cup Bundt pan.

2. In a large bowl, whisk together dry ingredients.

3. In a medium bowl, cream together butter and sugar until fluffy. (Use high speed on a handheld mixer, medium-high on a stand mixer.) Add eggs, 1 at a time, blending well between each addition. Stir in vanilla extract and orange zest. Add half of the dry ingredients; mix to combine. Add half of the orange juice; mix to combine. Add remaining dry ingredients and orange juice; mix batter for 1 minute.

4. Using a wooden spoon, stir in chocolate chips.

5. Spread batter evenly into prepared pan. Bake for 1 hour to 1 hour 15 minutes or until a tester inserted near the center comes out clean.

6. Remove pan from oven and set on a wire rack to cool, 10 minutes. Turn cake out onto rack to cool completely.

7. Dust the top of the cake with confectioners' sugar, if desired.

Makes one 10-inch Bundt cake

Classic
Chocolate Cake

During one of my cooking classes, a student took one bite of this cake and proclaimed, "This is just like a mix!" Many bakers would be insulted to be told their beloved recipe tastes like a box mix. Not me! I knew exactly what she meant: Cake mixes are moist with plenty of flavor, just like this cake.

Vegetable shortening, for pan
Cocoa powder, for pan

DRY INGREDIENTS
1 cup white rice flour
1/2 cup cornstarch
1/4 cup sweet rice flour
1 cup unsweetened cocoa powder
1 1/2 teaspoons baking powder
1 1/2 teaspoons baking soda
2 cups granulated sugar
1 teaspoon salt
1 teaspoon xanthan gum

WET INGREDIENTS
2 large eggs
1 cup milk
1/2 cup vegetable oil
2 teaspoons vanilla extract
1 cup very hot water

1. Preheat oven to 350°F. Grease and sprinkle cocoa powder on two 9-inch round cake pans or one 9x13-inch pan, or line 24 muffin cups with paper liners.

2. In a large bowl, whisk together the dry ingredients.

3. Add eggs, milk, oil, and vanilla. Using an electric mixer, beat for 2 minutes at medium speed. Turn mixer to low. Add hot water and mix for an additional minute.

4. Pour batter into prepared pans. Bake. For two 9-inch round pans, bake for 30 to 35 minutes. For a 9x13-inch pan, bake for 45 minutes. For cupcakes, bake for 18 to 20 minutes. A tester inserted into the center of any of the cakes should come out clean.

5. Remove pan(s) from the oven. Allow cake(s) to cool for 10 minutes in the pan. Turn out onto a wire rack to cool completely.

6. Once cake is cool, ice as desired.

Makes one 9x13 cake, one 9-inch layer cake, or 2 dozen cupcakes

Mile-High Chocolate Birthday Cake

When I envision my ideal birthday cake, this is it! Three wonderfully rich chocolate layers, filled and iced with silky buttercream.

Vegetable shortening, for pans
Cocoa powder, for pans

DRY INGREDIENTS
3 cups white rice flour
1 cup sweet rice flour
1/4 cup potato starch
1/4 cup cornstarch
3 cups granulated sugar
1/2 cup unsweetened cocoa powder
1 1/2 teaspoons salt
1 tablespoon baking soda

WET INGREDIENTS
2 large eggs
1 cup vegetable oil
3 cups water or cold coffee
1 tablespoon vanilla extract

Buttercream icing or chocolate buttercream
    icing (see recipes, page 181)

1. Preheat oven to 350°F. Grease three 8-inch round cake pans; dust pans lightly with cocoa powder (or spray with nonstick cooking spray).

2. In a very large bowl, whisk together dry ingredients. Add wet ingredients and mix for 1 minute. (Use medium speed on a handheld mixer or medium-low speed on a stand mixer.) If using a handheld mixer, be sure to scrape to the bottom of the bowl to ensure all the dry ingredients are fully incorporated.

3. Divide the batter evenly among the pans, filling each pan about halfway. Bake 35 to 40 minutes or until tester inserted into the center of cakes comes out clean.

4. Remove pans from the oven and place on wire racks to cool, 3 minutes. Turn cakes out onto a rack to cool completely.

5. Fill and frost with buttercream icing.

Makes 12 mile-high slices

Old Fashioned Spice Cake

This cake is moist and fragrant with my favorite spices—cinnamon, ginger, nutmeg, and clove—but it is not complete without cream cheese icing!

Vegetable shortening, for pan(s)
White rice flour, for pan(s)

DRY INGREDIENTS
3/4 cup white rice flour
3/4 cup brown rice flour
1/2 cup packed dark brown sugar
1/2 cup granulated sugar
1/2 cup cornstarch
1/4 cup tapioca starch
1/2 teaspoon xanthan gum
1/2 teaspoon salt
2 teaspoons baking soda
2 1/2 teaspoons ground cinnamon
1 teaspoon ground ginger
1/2 teaspoon ground nutmeg
1/4 teaspoon ground cloves

WET INGREDIENTS
2 large eggs
1/2 cup vegetable oil
1 1/2 cups buttermilk

Cream cheese icing (see recipe, page 183)

1. Preheat oven to 350°F. Grease and rice flour two 8-inch round pans or one 9x13-inch pan.

2. In a small bowl, whisk together dry ingredients.

3. In a large bowl, whisk together wet ingredients. Add dry ingredients. Using an electric mixer, mix for 2 minutes on medium speed.

4. Pour batter into prepared pans. Bake 35 to 40 minutes for 8-inch pans or 40 to 45 minutes for 9x13 inch pan. A tester inserted into the center of the cake should come out clean.

5. Allow cake to cool in the pan(s) for about 5 minutes before turning onto a wire rack to cool completely.

6. Ice cooled cake with cream cheese icing.

Makes one 8-inch layer cake or one 9x13-inch cake

Classic
Yellow Cake

1-eggs
1/2 c. oil or apple sauce

This was one of the hardest recipe for me to create. For long time (honestly, several years) the perfect yellow cake evaded me. I wanted something moist, with a nice crumb and delicate texture. After many attempts I finally created this recipe. It is moist! And tender! And delicious!

Gluten-free nonstick cooking spray

DRY INGREDIENTS

1 cup plus 2 tablespoons white rice flour

1 cup cornstarch

2 teaspoons baking powder

1 teaspoon xanthan gum

1 teaspoon salt

WET INGREDIENTS

1 cup (2 sticks) butter, softened

1 cup granulated sugar

4 large eggs

1/2 cup milk

2 teaspoons vanilla extract

1. Preheat oven to 350°F. Grease two 8-inch round pans or one 9x13-inch pan, or line 24 muffin cups with paper liners.

2. In a medium bowl, whisk together dry ingredients.

3. In another medium bowl, cream together butter and sugar until light and fluffy, about 30 seconds. (Use high speed on handheld mixer, medium-high on stand mixer.) Add eggs and beat for an additional 15 seconds. Mixture will be very fluffy. Add dry ingredients and mix until combined. Add milk and vanilla extract. Blend until batter is thoroughly combined and fluffy.

4. Pour batter into prepared pans. For 8-inch rounds, divide batter evenly between two pans. For the 9x13-inch pan, spread batter evenly into prepared pan. For cupcakes, fill muffin cups 1/2 full.

5. Bake until a tester inserted into the center of the cake comes out clean: For 8-inch rounds about 25 to 30; for 9x13-inch pan about 35 to 40 minutes; for cupcakes about 20 to 25 minutes.

6. Remove pan(s) from oven and place on wire racks to cool, 5 minutes. Transfer cake(s) directly onto racks to cool completely.

7. Ice as desired.

Makes one 8-inch layer cake, one 9x13-inch cake, or 2 dozen cupcakes

Hummingbird Cake

While flipping through an old cookbook, I came upon a recipe for hummingbird cake. Made with pineapples, bananas, and pecans, it sounded unusual. It's impossible to describe the flavor, so you'll just have to try it. I promise everyone will be humming around for another piece.

Vegetable shortening, for pan(s)
White rice flour, for pan(s)

DRY INGREDIENTS
2 cups white rice flour
1/2 cup sweet rice flour
1/4 cup cornstarch
1/4 cup tapioca starch
1 3/4 cups granulated sugar
1 teaspoon baking soda
1/2 teaspoon salt
1/2 teaspoon xanthan gum
2 teaspoons ground cinnamon

WET INGREDIENTS
1 cup vegetable oil
3 large eggs
1 teaspoon vanilla extract
1 (8-ounce) can crushed pineapple with juice
2 cups diced bananas, very ripe (about 3 medium bananas)
1 cup chopped pecans

Confectioners' sugar, for dusting (optional)
Cream cheese icing (optional; see recipe, page 183)

1. Preheat oven to 350°F. Grease and rice flour a 12-cup Bundt pan or three 8-inch round cake pans.

2. In a large bowl, whisk together dry ingredients.

3. Add oil, eggs, and vanilla; mix until smooth. (Use medium speed on a handheld or stand mixer.) At this point, the batter will be very stiff, almost like cookie dough.

4. Add pineapple with juice, bananas, and pecans. Mix until combined. (Use medium speed on a handheld or stand mixer.)

5. Spread batter into prepared pan(s). Bake Bundt cake for about 1 hour, layer cakes for 35 to 40 minutes, or until a tester inserted near the center of the cake comes out clean.

6. Remove pan(s) from the oven and place on a wire rack to cool, 15 minutes. Turn cake out onto rack to cool completely.

7. Dust with confectioners' sugar for the Bundt cake, or fill and ice with cream cheese icing for the round cake.

Makes one 10-inch Bundt cake or one 8-inch layer cake

Applesauce Cake

This wonderful cake recipe comes from Sherri R. of Mount Airy, North Carolina. This is an ideal spring recipe. The cake combines raisins, nuts, applesauce, and even maraschino cherries. It isn't quite a fruit-cake and it isn't exactly a light applesauce cake. It holds onto the wonderful spicy richness of winter, yet has a delightful light texture.

Vegetable shortening, for pans
White rice flour, for pans

DRY INGREDIENTS
1 1/2 cups white rice flour
1/2 cup sweet rice flour
1/2 cup cornstarch
1/2 teaspoon xanthan gum
1 1/2 teaspoons ground allspice
1 1/2 teaspoons baking soda
3/4 teaspoon salt

WET INGREDIENTS
1 1/2 cups golden raisins
3/4 cup vegetable shortening
1 1/2 cups granulated sugar
2 large eggs
1 1/2 cups unsweetened applesauce
3/4 cup chopped pecans
1 cup maraschino cherries, drained, halved, and
    patted dry with a paper towel

Confectioners' sugar, for dusting (optional)

1. Preheat oven to 325°F. Grease and rice flour a 12-cup Bundt pan.

2. In a medium bowl, whisk together dry ingredients. Remove about 1/2 cup of the dry ingredients.

3. In a separate bowl, toss the raisins with the reserved 1/2 cup dry ingredients.

4. In a large bowl, cream together shortening and sugar, about 30 seconds. (Use medium-high speed with a handheld mixer, medium speed with a stand mixer.) Add eggs and blend until smooth. Add dry ingredients and applesauce and blend for 1 minute. (Use medium speed with a handheld mixer, medium-low speed with a stand mixer.) Using a wooden spoon, stir in raisins, pecans, and cherries.

5. Pour batter evenly into the prepared pan and bake for 1 hour to 1 hour and 20 minutes, or until a tester inserted into the center of the cake comes out clean.

6. Remove pan from oven and place on a wire rack to cool, 7 minutes. Turn cake out onto rack to cool completely.

7. Dust with confectioners' sugar, if desired.

Makes one 10-inch Bundt cake

Pineapple Upside Down Cake

This cake has been around since the 1920s and for good reason. The flavors of the caramelized pineapples and brown sugar syrup marry perfectly with yellow cake.

DRY INGREDIENTS
1/2 cup white rice flour
1/4 cup sweet rice flour
1/4 cup potato starch
1/2 teaspoon baking powder
1/2 teaspoon salt

WET INGREDIENTS
5 tablespoons butter, melted
1/2 cup packed dark brown sugar
1 (20-ounce) can pineapple rings, drained with
   juice reserved
12 maraschino cherries
20 pecan or walnut halves
2 large eggs
2/3 cup granulated sugar
1 1/2 teaspoons vanilla extract

1. Preheat oven to 350°F.

2. In a medium bowl, whisk together dry ingredients.

3. Pour butter evenly into a 9-inch round cake pan. Sprinkle brown sugar evenly over the melted butter and arrange the pineapple rings on top. Place the cherries in the centers of the pineapple rings, and nestle the nuts between the pineapple rings.

4. In a large bowl, beat the eggs and sugar for 3 minutes. (Use high speed on a handheld mixer, medium-high speed on a stand mixer.) Add the dry ingredients, 1/2 cup of the reserved pineapple juice, and the vanilla; mix until a batter forms; the batter will be thin.

5. Pour the batter evenly over the pineapple rings. Bake the cake for 30 to 35 minutes or until a tester inserted into the center of the cake comes out clean.

6. Remove pan from the oven and place on a wire rack to cool, 5 minutes. Place a serving plate over the cake pan. Using both hands, carefully flip the cake pan over onto the serving plate. Carefully remove the cake pan and allow the cake to cool completely. (You might need to rearrange some of the fruit that moved during baking.)

Serves 8 to 10

Coconut Layer Cake

Three layers high, piled with light, marshmallow icing and covered with coconut, this cake looks like it belongs in a magazine. Not just a pretty face, it contains coconut both in the cake and in the icing.

Vegetable shortening, for pans
White rice flour, for pans

DRY INGREDIENTS
3 cups white rice flour
1/2 cup sweet rice flour
1/2 cup cornstarch
1 teaspoon xanthan gum
2 cups granulated sugar
2 tablespoons baking powder
2 teaspoons salt

WET INGREDIENTS
1 cup vegetable shortening
2 cups milk
4 large eggs
2 teaspoons vanilla extract

1 cup sweetened flaked coconut
Marshmallow icing (see recipe, page 182)

1. Preheat oven to 350°F. Grease and rice flour three 8-inch round cake pans.

2. In a large bowl, mix dry and wet ingredients, 2 minutes. Batter will be smooth and thick. Stir in coconut gently with a wooden spoon.

3. Pour batter into prepared pans, smoothing with a rubber spatula. Bake 25 minutes or until cakes spring back to the touch.

4. Allow cakes to cool in pans 5 minutes, then turn them out onto a wire rack to cool completely.

5. Place one cooled cake onto a serving plate. Spread a layer of icing on top. Sprinkle a thick layer of coconut over the icing. Repeat with remaining 2 cake layers.

6. Spread the remaining icing over sides of the cake. Sprinkle all remaining coconut onto sides and top of cake.

Serves 10

Brown Sugar Cupcakes

These cupcakes have such a pleasant molasses-vanilla flavor they don't really require icing. Make these cupcakes whenever you want to get in and out of the kitchen fast.

DRY INGREDIENTS
1 cup white rice flour
1/2 cup cornstarch
1/2 cup sweet rice flour
1 teaspoon baking soda
1/2 teaspoon salt
1/2 teaspoon xanthan gum

WET INGREDIENTS
1/2 cup vegetable shortening
1 cup packed dark brown sugar
1 large egg
1 cup milk
2 teaspoons vanilla extract

1. Preheat oven to 375°F. Line 12 muffin cups with paper liners.

2. In a medium bowl, whisk together dry ingredients.

3. In a large bowl, cream together shortening and brown sugar, 25 seconds. Add egg, milk, and vanilla. Blend until combined. (Use medium-high speed on handheld and stand mixers.) Add dry ingredients and mix until well blended.

4. Fill prepared muffin cups about two-thirds full. Bake for 15 to 20 minutes or until a tester inserted into the center of the cupcakes comes out clean.

5. Remove pan from the oven and set on a wire rack to cool, 5 minutes. Turn cupcakes out onto rack to cool completely.

Makes 1 dozen cupcakes

Poke Cake

Here is one of those home-style classics that everyone loves! It's a classic yellow cake with Jell-O "poked" into it! You can omit the Jell-O if you wish. The traditional topping is whipped cream, but you can use buttercream, or go without topping.

Vegetable shortening, for the pan
White rice flour, for the pan

DRY INGREDIENTS
1 1/2 cups white rice flour
3/4 cup cornstarch
1/4 cup sweet rice flour
1/2 teaspoon xanthan gum
3/4 teaspoon salt
2 1/2 teaspoons baking powder

WET INGREDIENTS
3/4 cup (1 1/2 sticks) butter, softened
1 3/4 cups granulated sugar
4 large eggs
2 large egg yolks
1 1/2 cups milk
2 teaspoons vanilla extract

For the Poke
1 (3-ounce) package Jell-O (cherry, strawberry, or raspberry, or your choice)
1 cup boiling water
1/2 cup cold water

Whipped cream, or buttercream icing (see recipe, page 181) (optional)

1. Preheat oven to 350°F. Grease and rice flour a 9x13-inch pan.

2. In a medium bowl, whisk together the dry ingredients.

3. In a large bowl, cream together butter and sugar until light and fluffy, about 45 seconds. (Use high speed on a handheld mixer, medium-high speed on a stand mixer.) Add the eggs and yolks to the butter mixture, 1 at a time, beating well after each addition. Add half of the dry ingredients and blend until combined. (Use medium-high speed with a handheld mixer, medium speed with a stand mixer.) Add milk and vanilla; blend for 45 seconds. Add remaining dry ingredients and blend until smooth.

4. Pour batter into prepared cake pan. Bake for about 35 minutes or until a tester inserted into the center of the cake comes out clean.

5. Remove pan from the oven and place on wire rack to cool completely. Use a fork to pierce cake all over, creating small holes.

6. Combine boiling water and Jell-O. Stir until Jell-O is dissolved. Add cold water and stir.

7. Pour Jell-O mixture over the cake.

8. Once cake has absorbed the Jell-O, refrigerate for 4 hours before serving.

9. Top cake with whipped cream, if desired.

Makes 9 to 12 servings

Easy
Chocolate Trifle

After my classic chocolate cake recipe was published, I received a slew of e-mails from readers asking what else they could do with this wonderful cake. Here is one answer: Make a trifle!

1 cup heavy cream
1/4 cup confectioners' sugar
1 classic chocolate cake (see recipe, page 160),
     baked in a 9x13-inch cake pan
2 (4-serving-size) packages regular or instant
     chocolate pudding, prepared according to
     package directions and chilled
1 cup toasted slivered almonds (optional)

1. Whip heavy cream and confectioners' sugar together to form stiff peaks. (Use high speed on handheld or stand mixer.)

2. Cut cooled cake into 1/2-inch cubes.

3. In a glass trifle bowl, spread one-third of the cake cubes. Spoon one-third of the chocolate pudding over cake cubes. Spoon one-third of the whipped cream over the pudding. (If using toasted nuts, sprinkle one-third of the nuts over the top of the whipped cream.) Repeat until all ingredients are used.

4. Serve immediately or refrigerate until ready to serve.

Serves 16

Baker's Note

If you are using cook-and-serve pudding, you might want to make the pudding the night before. To prevent a skin from forming on your pudding, press a piece of plastic wrap on its surface. Store in the refrigerator overnight.

Trifle Variations

Coconut: Use coconut cream pudding in place of the chocolate pudding. Substitute the slivered almonds with 1 cup toasted coconut. To toast coconut, preheat oven to 350°F; place 1 cup sweetened, flaked coconut on a baking sheet and toast, stirring occasionally, for 5 to 9 minutes, until lightly browned. Toasting time will vary greatly depending on the sweetness and moisture content of your coconut. Be sure to keep an eye on the coconut as it toasts.

Banana: Use banana cream or vanilla pudding in place of the chocolate pudding. Substitute the slivered almonds with 1 1/2 cups thinly sliced bananas (about 2 large bananas).

Boston Cream Pie

This recipe is the perfect antidote for a blah winter day. Made in three steps, it will give you something fun to do. And when it is done, it's so pretty you will forget that it gets dark at around 5:00 pm. The filling needs to set up for at least four hours. I usually make the filling the day before I plan to make this pie.

For the Filling

2/3 cup milk

1/3 cup granulated sugar

3/4 cup heavy cream

1/4 cup cornstarch

1 large egg yolk (save the egg white for the cake)

2 teaspoons vanilla extract

For the Cake

DRY INGREDIENTS

1/4 cup vegetable shortening, plus more for pan

3/4 cup white rice flour, plus more for pan

2 tablespoons sweet rice flour

2 tablespoons cornstarch

1/4 teaspoon xanthan gum

1/2 cup granulated sugar

1 teaspoon salt

11/2 teaspoons baking powder

WET INGREDIENTS

1/2 cup milk

1 large egg

1 large egg white

1 teaspoon vanilla extract

For the Icing

4 ounces dark chocolate, coarsely chopped

1/2 cup heavy cream

1. Prepare the filling: In a medium saucepan over medium-high heat, combine the milk and sugar. Heat, stirring, until sugar is dissolved.

2. In a small bowl, vigorously whisk together the heavy cream, cornstarch, and egg yolk.

3. Reduce the heat under the milk and sugar to low. While whisking the hot milk, very slowly pour the heavy cream mixture into the saucepan.

4. Increase heat to medium. Whisk mixture constantly until it thickens, about 2 1/2 minutes. Remove filling from heat, continue to whisk mixture for an additional minute, then whisk vanilla into slightly cooled filling.

5. Pour filling into a large bowl. Place a piece of plastic wrap directly on the surface of the filling. (This will prevent a skin from forming.)

6. Refrigerate filling for 4 hours or overnight.

7. Prepare the cake: Preheat oven to 350°F. Grease and rice flour one 9-inch round cake pan.

8. In a medium bowl, mix all ingredients for 2 minutes; batter will be thick. (Use medium-high speed on handheld and stand mixers.)

9. Pour batter into pan and bake for 25 minutes or until a tester inserted into the center of the cake comes out clean.

10. Remove cake from oven and place on a wire rack to cool in the pan, 5 minutes. Turn cake out onto cooling rack to cool completely.

11. Prepare the icing: Place chopped chocolate into a large bowl.

12. In saucepan or microwave-safe bowl, bring cream to a boil; remove from heat.

13. Pour boiled cream over chocolate. Stir, using a wooden spoon, until chocolate melts and no lumps remain. Allow icing to cool for 8 minutes.

To Assemble

1. Using a serrated knife, slice the cooled cake in half horizontally. Gently remove the top portion of the cake. Set aside.

2. Spread all of the filling onto the bottom half of the cake. Top with reserved cake layer.

3. Ladle lightly cooled icing onto the cake. Refrigerate until ready to serve.

Serves 6 to 8

German Chocolate Cake

German chocolate cake isn't German at all; it's a purely American creation. The recipe first appeared in a Texas newspaper in 1957. The chocolate used in the recipe was Baker's German's Sweet Chocolate—named for Samuel German. So, the cake is named for a person, not a country!

Gluten-free nonstick cooking spray

WET INGREDIENTS

1 (4-ounce) package Baker's German's Sweet
    Chocolate
1 cup (2 sticks) butter, softened
1 3/4 cups granulated sugar
4 large eggs
1 cup buttermilk
1/2 cup water
1 teaspoon vanilla extract

DRY INGREDIENTS

1 cup white rice flour
1/2 cup sweet rice flour
1/2 cup cornstarch
1 teaspoon baking soda
1/2 teaspoon xanthan gum
1/4 teaspoon salt

German Chocolate Icing (see recipe facing page)

1. Preheat oven to 350°F. Grease a 9x13-inch baking pan with cooking spray.

2. In a microwave-safe bowl, melt chocolate. (Microwave chocolate for 20 seconds, then remove the bowl from the microwave and stir. Repeat until completely melted.) Set aside to cool.

3. In a medium bowl, whisk together dry ingredients.

4. In a large bowl, cream together butter and sugar until light and fluffy, about 1 minute. (Use medium-high speed with a handheld mixer, medium speed with a stand mixer.) In a slow and steady steam, add the chocolate. Add the eggs, 1 at a time, mixing well after each addition. Add half the dry ingredients; mix until combined. (Use medium-low speed on a handheld mixer, low speed on a stand mixer.) Add the buttermilk and mix until combined. Add remaining dry ingredients and mix until combined. Finally, add the water and vanilla; mix for 1 minute.

5. Spread batter into prepared pan. Bake for 35 to 45 minutes or until a tester inserted into the center of the cake comes out clean.

6. Remove pan from oven and set on a wire rack to cool, 5 minutes. Turn cake out onto wire rack to cool completely.

7. Spread icing on cake.

Makes one 9x13-inch cake

German Chocolate Icing

1 tablespoon cornstarch
1 cup evaporated milk
1/2 cup granulated sugar
1/2 cup packed dark brown sugar
4 large egg yolks, at room temperature

1/4 cup (1/2 stick) butter, softened
1/2 teaspoon salt
1 teaspoon vanilla extract
1/2 cup chopped pecans
1 cup sweetened, flaked coconut

1. In a medium saucepan, whisk together cornstarch, evaporated milk, granulated sugar, brown sugar, egg yolks, butter, and salt. Cook mixture, stirring constantly, over medium heat until mixture boils. Remove mixture from heat and stir for 1 minute. Add vanilla extract, chopped pecans, and coconut. Stir to combine.

2. Allow icing to cool for 10 minutes or until slightly warmer than room temperature before using.

Strawberry Cake

Several readers requested a box-like strawberry cake. Here it is! Perfect for kids, this cake is pink—courtesy of the Jell-O and strawberry extract. This cake does not contain fresh berries: It's simply not that type of cake. It's the kind of cake that makes great cupcakes or a picture perfect birthday cake.

Vegetable shortening, for pan
White rice flour, for pan

DRY INGREDIENTS
2 cups white rice flour
1/2 cup sweet rice flour
1/2 cup potato starch
2 1/2 teaspoons baking powder
1/2 teaspoon salt
1 (3-ounce) package strawberry Jell-O

WET INGREDIENTS
2/3 cup butter or margarine, softened
1 1/4 cups granulated sugar
2 large eggs
2 teaspoons strawberry extract
1 1/4 cups milk

1. Preheat oven to 350°F. Grease and rice flour two 8-inch cake pans or one 9x13-inch pan, or line 24 muffin cups with paper liners.

2. In a medium bowl, whisk together dry ingredients.

3. In a large bowl, cream together butter and sugar until light and fluffy, about 45 seconds. (Use high speed on a handheld mixer, medium-high speed on a stand mixer.) Add eggs and strawberry extract to the creamed mixture and beat until thoroughly mixed.

4. Reduce speed to medium-low and add half the dry ingredients to the butter mixture; mix for 30 seconds. Add half the milk; mix for 30 seconds. Add the remaining dry ingredients; mix for 30 seconds. Add remaining milk; mix until combined.

5. Pour batter into prepared pan(s). Bake cake(s) until a tester inserted into the center comes out clean. (30 to 40 minutes for 8-inch pans, 45 minutes for 9x13-inch pan, or 25 minutes for cupcakes.)

6. Remove cakes from oven and allow to cool in the pans for 5 minutes. Turn cakes out onto a cooling rack to cool completely. Ice as desired.

Makes one 8-inch layer cake, one 9x13-inch cake, or 2 dozen cupcakes

Basic Buttercream

This is the icing I turn to again and again. It's so simple to make; I prepare it while my cake cools.

DRY INGREDIENTS
4 cups (1 pound) confectioners' sugar
1/2 teaspoon salt

WET INGREDIENTS
1 cup (2 sticks) butter, softened
1/4 cup milk
2 teaspoons vanilla extract

1. In a medium bowl, whisk together dry ingredients.

2. In a large bowl, cream butter until light and fluffy, about 30 seconds. (Use high speed on a handheld or stand mixer.) Add dry ingredients and cream together for 10 seconds. Pour milk and vanilla evenly over the icing. Blend, on low speed, for 45 seconds or until smooth and creamy.

Makes 3 cups of icing

Basic Chocolate Buttercream

DRY INGREDIENTS
4 cups (1 pound) confectioners' sugar
3/4 cup Dutch process cocoa powder
1/2 teaspoon salt

WET INGREDIENTS
1 cup (2 sticks) butter, softened
1/4 cup milk
2 teaspoons vanilla extract

1. In a medium bowl, whisk together dry ingredients.

2. In a large bowl, cream butter until light and fluffy, about 30 seconds. (Use high speed on a handheld or stand mixer.) Add dry ingredients and cream together for 10 seconds. Pour milk and vanilla evenly over the icing. Blend, on low speed, for 45 seconds or until smooth and creamy.

Makes 3 cups of icing

Marshmallow
Icing

4 large egg whites
1 1/4 cups granulated sugar
1 cup shredded sweetened coconut

1. Place egg whites and sugar in the top of a double boiler set over simmering water.

2. Whisk egg whites and sugar together until sugar is dissolved and egg whites are warm to the touch.

3. Pour egg whites into a clean medium bowl.

4. Using a handheld or stand mixer, whip egg whites on high speed for about 7 minutes or until icing is thick, shiny, and cool to the touch. (Icing should hold firm peaks.)

5. Using a rubber spatula, fold coconut into whipped icing.

Baker's Note

You will notice in step three of the icing recipe, I note that a clean bowl must be used. Egg whites will not whip in the presence of oil. Therefore, your bowl—and whisk attachment—must be completely grease-free or you won't end up with a thick icing.

This icing recipe calls for a double boiler. To create a double boiler, fill a saucepan with about 2 inches of water. Set a heatproof bowl into the saucepan. Be sure the bottom of the bowl does not touch the water. (It should hang snugly in the saucepan.) Heat the water over medium heat. Do not boil the water. Simmering water is all you need. Take care not to burn yourself when removing the bowl from the saucepan.

Makes 4 to 5 cups of icing

Cream Cheese Icing

WET INGREDIENTS

8 ounces cream cheese, at room temperature
1/2 cup (1 stick) butter, softened
1 teaspoon vanilla extract

DRY INGREDIENTS

4 cups (1 pound) confectioners' sugar

In a large bowl, combine cream cheese, butter, and vanilla; cream until smooth. (Use high speed on hand-held and stand mixers.) Add confectioners' sugar; beat until light and fluffy.

Makes about 3 cups of icing

Pies

Piecrust

People give piecrust too much power. In fact, one of the biggest Thanksgiving fears is having to make and roll out homemade piecrust. Here is the lowdown: Start with cold butter. Use a fork or a pastry cutter to blend in the butter/shortening. When the butter/shortening is incorporated enough, the flour mixture will hold together when squeezed and no large nuggets of butter/shortening will remain. If you have a food processor, you can also use that to incorporate the butter.

Once that step is out of the way, add the water. Use a fork or pastry cutter to blend in the water; mix until a dough forms. If the dough looks dry, a very common problem, add more water. That's it! Just remember to wrap the dough with plastic wrap and store in the refrigerator.

Now, let's tackle rolling out the dough. If you try to roll cold piecrust it will break apart. When it comes time to roll out the dough, take it out of the refrigerator fifteen minutes before you plan to roll it out. Place a large piece of parchment paper or plastic wrap on your work area. Put the dough down in the middle of the work area. Generously white rice flour the top of the dough round. Cover dough with another piece of parchment or plastic wrap. Roll the piecrust out to about a 1/4-inch thickness. Remove the top piece of parchment or plastic wrap. Flip your pie pan upside down in the middle of the rolled-out crust. Slip your hand under the crust and quickly flip the crust into the pan. Once the pan is right side up, slowly pull the parchment paper or plastic wrap off of the crust. Flute or crimp the edges of your crust as desired.

Baker's Note

To make sure your piecrust is large enough for the pan, place the pie pan upside down on your rolled-out dough. The crust should be about 2 inches larger than the perimeter of your pan.

Either butter or vegetable shortening can be used with excellent results in my piecrust recipes. Butter provides excellent flavor while shortening yields the flakiest crust. Your personal preference should dictate your use. You can even use half butter and half shortening to get the best of both!

Single Piecrust

DRY INGREDIENTS

1/2 cup white rice flour, plus more for dusting

1/4 cup cornstarch

1/4 cup potato starch

1 1/2 teaspoons granulated sugar

1/4 teaspoon salt

WET INGREDIENTS

1/4 cup (1/2 stick) cold butter, cut into pieces
   (or 1/4 cup solid vegetable shortening)

1 large egg

1 to 2 tablespoons cold water

Double Piecrust

DRY INGREDIENTS

1 cup white rice flour, plus more for dusting

1/2 cup cornstarch

1/2 cup potato starch

1 tablespoon granulated sugar

1/2 teaspoon salt

WET INGREDIENTS

1/2 cup (1 stick) cold butter, cut into pieces
   (or 1/2 cup solid vegetable shortening)

1 large egg

3 to 4 tablespoons cold water

1. In a large bowl, whisk together dry ingredients.

2. Using a fork or pastry cutter, work cold butter or shortening into flour mixture. Add egg and water. If dough is dry, add more water 1 teaspoon at a time. Stir until a dough forms.

3. Wrap the dough in plastic wrap and chill for 1 hour. (If making a double crust, divide dough in half and wrap each half separately.)

4. Remove dough from the refrigerator and place on the counter for 15 minutes.

Cookie Crust

1 1/2 cups crushed gluten-free cookies (graham
   crackers, vanilla, or chocolate)

6 tablespoons butter, melted

2 tablespoons sugar (or more to taste)

1. Preheat oven to 350°F. In a medium bowl, combine all ingredients.

2. Press the mixture into a 9-inch pie pan. Crust should cover the bottom and sides of pan.

3. Bake the crust for about 10 minutes. Allow to cool before using.

Apple Pie

Dough for 1 double piecrust recipe, chilled
(see recipe, page 187)

6 cups thinly sliced peeled apples (Granny Smith
or another tart apple, or a combination of tart
and sweet apples)

3/4 cup plus 2 tablespoons granulated sugar

1 tablespoon cornstarch

1 teaspoon ground cinnamon

1/4 teaspoon ground nutmeg

1 tablespoon freshly squeezed lemon juice

1 egg yolk, lightly beaten

Whipped cream or vanilla ice cream, for serving
(optional)

1. Preheat oven to 375°F. Place a sheet of plastic wrap or parchment paper on a work surface and place half the dough on it; cover with another sheet of plastic or parchment. Roll out half of the pie dough to a 12 1/2-inch circle. Transfer dough into a 9-inch pie plate. Trim dough so that it only hangs over the edge about 1/2 inch. Place the crust in the refrigerator while you prepare the filling.

2. In a large bowl, using a wooden spoon, mix together the apples, 3/4 cup sugar, cornstarch, cinnamon, nutmeg, and lemon juice.

3. Roll remaining pie dough to a 12 1/2-inch round.

4. Remove bottom crust from the refrigerator and mound the filling into the crust.

5. Drape the remaining pie dough on top of the apple filling. Using a fork or your fingers, crimp the edges of the pie dough together. Brush the top of the pie with the egg yolk and sprinkle with 2 tablespoons sugar. Using a sharp knife, cut several small slits into the top crust.

6. Bake for 45 to 50 minutes or until crust is lightly brown and filling is bubbling.

7. Remove pie from the oven and place on a wire rack to cool. Serve with whipped cream or vanilla ice cream.

Serves 8

Pumpkin Pie

To make a perfect pumpkin pie, don't use a pumpkin-pie spice blend; for some reason, it lends a somewhat funky flavor to pumpkin pie. Take the time to measure out the individual spices; it really does make a difference.

Dough for 1 single piecrust, chilled
   (see recipe, page 187)
1 (15-ounce) can pure pumpkin (not pumpkin
   pie filling)
1 (12-ounce) can evaporated milk
3/4 cup packed dark brown sugar
2 large eggs

1 1/2 teaspoons ground cinnamon
1/2 teaspoon ground ginger
1/2 teaspoon salt
1/4 teaspoon ground cloves
1/4 teaspoon ground nutmeg

Whipped cream, for serving (optional)

1. Preheat oven to 350°F. Place a sheet of plastic wrap or parchment paper on a work surface and place half the dough on it; cover with another sheet of plastic or parchment. Roll out dough to a 12 1/2-inch circle and place in a 9-inch pie plate. Crimp the edges of the crust.

2. In a large bowl, combine remaining ingredients. Blend with a handheld or stand mixer at medium speed for 2 minutes. Pour mixture into prepared unbaked piecrust.

3. Bake for 45 minutes or just until the pie does not jiggle in the center.

4. Remove pie from oven and place on a wire rack to cool. Store pie in the refrigerator once it has cooled. Serve with whipped cream, if desired.

Serves 8

Blueberry Pie

I always freeze several pints of blueberries during the height of the season. Then, in the darkest days of winter, I pull them out of the freezer and make a blueberry pie. After sinking my teeth into that first bite of "winter blueberry pie," I am reminded that snow doesn't last forever and good things are to come.

Dough for 1 double piecrust, chilled
  (see recipe, page 187)
2 pints fresh blueberries, washed and picked over
3/4 cup plus 2 tablespoons granulated sugar
2 tablespoons cornstarch

2 tablespoons freshly squeezed lemon juice
1 teaspoon vanilla extract
1 egg yolk, lightly beaten

Whipped cream or vanilla ice cream, for serving
  (optional)

1. Preheat oven to 375°F. Place a sheet of plastic wrap or parchment paper on a work surface and place half the dough on it; cover with another sheet of plastic or parchment. Roll out dough to about a 12 1/2-inch circle. Transfer into 9-inch pie plate. Trim dough so that it only hangs over the edge about 1/2 inch. Place the crust in the refrigerator while you prepare the filling.

2. In a large bowl, using a wooden spoon, gently mix together the blueberries, 3/4 cup granulated sugar, cornstarch, lemon juice, and vanilla. Allow to stand for 5 minutes.

3. Roll out remaining pie dough to about a 12 1/2-inch circle.

4. Remove bottom piecrust from the refrigerator and spoon the blueberry filling into the crust.

5. Drape top crust on top of the blueberries. Using a fork or your fingers crimp the edges of the pie dough together. Brush the top of the pie with the egg yolk and sprinkle with the remaining 2 tablespoons sugar. Using a sharp knife, cut several small slits into the top crust.

6. Place a cookie sheet in the oven and place the pie on top of it. Bake for 45 to 50 minutes or until crust is lightly brown and filling is bubbling.

7. Remove pie from the oven and place on a wire rack to cool. Serve with whipped cream or vanilla ice cream, if desired.

Serves 8

Peach Pie

When making this pie, please use only the ripest, most fragrant peaches. Peach pie needs to scream "PEACH!" from the top of its lungs. If your peaches are underripe, the flavor just won't be as wonderful.

Dough for 1 double piecrust, chilled
    (see recipe, page 187)
8 to 10 ripe, medium peaches, peeled, pitted, and
    cut into 1/4-inch slices
21/2 tablespoons cornstarch
1/4 cup packed dark brown sugar
1/2 teaspoon ground nutmeg

1/4 teaspoon ground cinnamon
1 teaspoon vanilla extract
1/4 cup (1/2 stick) cold butter, cut into 8 pieces
1 egg yolk, lightly beaten
2 tablespoons granulated sugar

Whipped cream or vanilla ice cream, for serving
    (optional)

1. Preheat oven to 375°F. Place a sheet of plastic wrap or parchment paper on a work surface and place half the dough on it; cover with another sheet of plastic or parchment. Roll out dough to a 121/2-inch circle. Transfer into 9-inch diameter pie plate. Trim dough so that it only hangs over the edge about 1/2 inch. Place the crust in the refrigerator while you prepare the filling.

2. In a large bowl, using a wooden spoon, mix together the peaches, cornstarch, brown sugar, nutmeg, cinnamon, and vanilla.

3. Roll remaining pie dough out to a 121/2- inch circle.

4. Remove bottom crust from the refrigerator and mound the filling into the crust. Dot the top with the pieces of cold butter.

5. Drape the remaining pie dough on top of the peaches. Using a fork or your fingers, crimp the edges of the pie dough together. Brush the top with the egg yolk and sprinkle with 2 tablespoons sugar. Using a sharp knife, cut several small slits into the top crust.

6. Bake for 45 to 50 minutes or until crust is lightly brown and filling is bubbling.

7. Remove pie from the oven and place on a wire rack to cool. Serve with whipped cream or vanilla ice cream, if desired.

Serves 8

Lemon Meringue Pie

Most pies are a seasonal treat. But because lemons are available all year, you can make this pie whenever you are in the mood for it!

Dough for 1 single piecrust (see recipe, page 187)
1¼ cups granulated sugar
6 tablespoons cornstarch
1½ cups water

3 egg yolks
2 tablespoons butter
⅓ cup freshly squeezed lemon juice
Meringue (see recipe, below)

1. Preheat oven to 425°F. Place a sheet of plastic wrap on a work surface and place the dough on it; cover with another sheet of plastic wrap. Roll out dough to about a 12½-inch circle. Transfer into 9-inch pie plate. Trim dough.

2. Prick the bottom of the pie dough lightly with the tines of a fork. Bake for 10 to 12 minutes or until golden brown. Set aside.

3. In a medium saucepan combine sugar, cornstarch, and water. Cook over medium heat until thick and bubbling. Reduce to low heat and simmer for an additional 2 minutes.

4. Remove pan from heat. In a small bowl, whisk egg yolks until combined. Slowly whisk ½ cup of the hot filling into the yolks. Stir yolk mixture back into the pot. Cook for about 2 minutes, stirring frequently. Remove from heat, stir in butter. Add lemon juice slowly, mixing well.

5. Pour hot filling into prebaked piecrust.

6. Allow to cool thoroughly in the refrigerator.

7. Top with meringue. Place pie under broiler. (Set broiler to high and place on highest oven rack or directly into the broiler, depending on oven.) Bake until brown, about 2 to 3 minutes. (Watch pie closely; this step goes quickly!)

Meringue

4 egg whites
1 cup sugar

1. In the top of a double boiler set over simmering water, combine egg whites and sugar. Whisk egg whites until sugar is dissolved and mixture is hot.

2. Transfer mixture to an electric mixer and whip on high speed until smooth and glossy, about 10 minutes.

Serves 6

Whole Strawberry Pie

This recipe comes from Jan Entwistle, a friend of my mother's. Not only is this pie gorgeous, but it has a hidden surprise! Hiding beneath the layer of whole strawberries is a layer of cream cheese.

Dough for 1 single piecrust (see recipe, page 187)
   or cookie crust (see recipe, page 187)
3 ounces cream cheese
1/2 pint heavy cream
1 teaspoon vanilla extract

1 quart whole, fresh, ripe strawberries
1 cup granulated sugar
3 tablespoons cornstarch
3 tablespoons confectioners' sugar

1. Preheat oven to 425°F. Place a sheet of plastic wrap on a work surface and place the dough on it; cover with another sheet of plastic wrap. Roll out dough to about a 12 1/2-inch circle. Transfer into 9-inch pie plate. Trim dough.

2. Prick the bottom of the pie dough lightly with the tines of a fork. Bake for 10 to 12 minutes or until golden brown. Set aside.

3. In a small bowl, mix together the cream cheese with 2 tablespoons heavy cream and the vanilla. (Use medium-high speed for handheld and stand mixers.)

4. Spread mixture evenly on the bottom and sides of the prepared piecrust. Cut the tops off the strawberries and line pie with half of the strawberries, point side up.

5. In a small bowl, whisk together sugar and cornstarch with a fork.

6. Mash remaining strawberries in a small saucepan. Add the sugar and cornstarch mixture. Bring mixture to a boil and allow to boil for 2 minutes. Reduce heat to low heat and simmer for 10 minutes.

7. Pour mixture over prepared pie.

8. Chill pie in the refrigerator until set, about 4 hours.

9. In a small bowl, add confectioners' sugar to remaining cream. Whip to soft peaks. (Use high speed on handheld and stand mixers.) Serve pie with whipped cream.

Serves 6

Easy Banana Cream Pie

My mom's pies won so many ribbons at the local fair, they asked her to stop competing. So, when she said recently, "I made a quick banana cream pie," I listened. The pie was smooth, velvety, and had a pleasant vanilla flavor. After I told her I liked it, she revealed her secret: The filling was made using cook-and-serve pudding doctored with a splash of vanilla—it takes only about 10 minutes to make from crust to filling!

1¹/3 cups gluten-free "graham cracker" crumbs
(I used Health Valley rice bran crackers)
¹/4 cup (¹/2 stick) butter, melted
2 tablespoons granulated sugar
2 (3.4 ounce) packages vanilla cook-and-serve
pudding

3¹/2 cups milk
1 tablespoon vanilla extract
2 large very ripe bananas, sliced thin
1 cup heavy cream
¹/4 cup confectioners' sugar, or more to taste

1. Preheat oven to 350°F. In a small bowl, stir together the "graham cracker" crumbs, melted butter, and sugar. Press mixture into the bottom and sides of a 9-inch pie pan.

2. Bake for 8 to 10 minutes or until the edges just begin to brown.

3. Remove the crust from the oven and allow to cool completely.

4. In a medium saucepan, combine the pudding mix with the milk. Cook over medium heat, stirring constantly, until mixture comes to a boil. Remove from heat and allow to cool for 5 minutes. Add vanilla and stir to combine.

5. Line the bottom of the pie shell with half of the sliced bananas. Pour half of the pudding mixture over the sliced bananas. Arrange remaining bananas over the pudding. Pour the remaining pudding over the bananas. Place a piece of plastic wrap directly on the surface of the pie (this will prevent a skin from forming).

6. Refrigerate pie for 4 hours or overnight.

7. Whip cream together with confectioners' sugar until soft peaks form. (Use high speed on handheld and stand mixers.) Spread whipped cream over the top of the pie.

Serves 6

Sweet Potato
Pie

Roasted sweet potatoes, removed from their jackets and mashed, make the best filling for sweet potato pie. The roasting brings out their sweet, earthy flavor. Often, the night before I plan to make this pie, I throw a few sweet potatoes into the oven along with dinner. This way my sweet potatoes are ready to go and I don't have to turn on the oven just to roast them.

Dough for 1 single piecrust, chilled
   (see recipe, page 187)
3 cups mashed sweet potatoes (about 4 medium
   sweet potatoes)
3 large eggs
1 cup granulated sugar

1 cup heavy cream
$1/2$ teaspoon salt
2 teaspoons ground cinnamon
1 teaspoon ground nutmeg
$1/4$ teaspoon ground allspice

Whipped cream or ice cream (optional)

1. Preheat oven to 350°F. Place a sheet of plastic wrap or parchment paper on a work surface and place the dough on it; cover with another sheet of plastic or parchment. Roll out the dough to a 12-inch circle and place in a 9-inch pie pan. Trim and crimp the edges of the crust. Return crust to refrigerator.

2. In a medium bowl, combine remaining ingredients. Blend with a handheld or stand mixer at medium speed for 2 minutes.

3. Spread mixture into prepared piecrust. Filling will be thick.

4. Bake for 45 minutes or until filling is golden brown.

5. Remove pie from oven and place on a wire rack to cool completely. Store pie in the refrigerator.

Serves 6 to 8

Mincemeat
Pie

People who claim to hate mincemeat love my mother's mincemeat pie. However, much to her chagrin, I am not a mincemeat lover. I can't stand raisins. But I am no fool. I've seen too many people swoon over this recipe not to pass it on to you. (Don't worry. There is no meat in this mincemeat pie.)

4 large apples peeled, cored, and sliced into
   1/2-inch pieces (tart apples work best)
1/4 cup orange juice (preferably fresh squeezed)
1/2 cup packed dark brown sugar
1/2 cup raisins
1/2 cup chopped dried apricots
1/4 teaspoon salt
1/4 teaspoon ground cinnamon

1/4 teaspoon ground nutmeg
1/4 teaspoon ground cloves
11/2 teaspoons vanilla extract
2 tablespoons rum
Dough for 1 double piecrust, chilled
   (see recipe, page 187)
1 egg yolk, lightly beaten
2 tablespoons granulated sugar

1. Preheat oven to 350°F. Combine the apples, orange juice, brown sugar, raisins, apricots, salt, and spices in a medium saucepan. Cover and simmer over low heat for 30 minutes.

2. Remove cover and allow filling to cook until the liquid evaporates, about 5 to 10 minutes. Turn off heat and add rum. Allow filling to cool completely.

3. Place a sheet of plastic wrap or parchment paper on a work surface and place half the dough on it; cover with another sheet of plastic or parchment. Roll out half the dough to a 121/2-inch circle and place it in a 9-inch pie pan. Trim dough so it only hangs over pan 1/2 an inch.

4. Spoon filling into crust.

5. Roll out remaining dough and top pie. Crimp edges together.

6. Brush egg yolk over the top of the pie and sprinkle lightly with granulated sugar. Cut vents in top.

7. Bake for 45 minutes or until filling is bubbling and crust is golden brown.

8. Remove from the oven and place on a wire rack to cool.

Serves 6 to 8

Strawberry-Rhubarb Pie

If you've made the mistake of eating rhubarb fresh, I bet you still remember that tart, puckery flavor. It's almost like biting into a lemon. But baked rhubarb is amazing. It brings an unmistakable sweet-tart flavor.

2 cups sliced strawberries

3 cups 1-inch pieces rhubarb

3/4 cup plus 2 tablespoons granulated sugar, plus more as needed

1/4 teaspoon salt

1/4 teaspoon ground nutmeg

1 tablespoon cornstarch

Dough for 1 double piecrust, chilled (see recipe, page 187)

1 tablespoon cold butter, cut into small pieces

1 egg, lightly beaten

Whipped cream (optional)

1. Preheat oven to 350°F. In a large bowl, combine strawberries, rhubarb, 3/4 cup sugar, salt, nutmeg, and cornstarch. Allow filling to stand for 15 minutes.

2. Taste a little of the juice and adjust for sweetness. If you add more sugar, allow the filling to stand for an additional 10 minutes.

3. Place a sheet of plastic wrap or parchment paper on a work surface and place half the dough on it; cover with another sheet of plastic or parchment. Roll out the dough to a 12 1/2-inch circle and place in a 9-inch pie pan. Trim crust so 1/2 inch hangs over edge of pan.

4. Spoon the filling into the crust. Dot the top of the filling with the pieces of cold butter.

5. Roll out remaining pie dough and drape it over the filling. Crimp the edges. Brush the top of the pie with the beaten egg. Generously sprinkle 2 tablespoons granulated sugar over the top of the pie. Cut vents in top of pie.

6. Line a baking sheet with foil; place pie on baking sheet. Bake for 45 minutes or until the filling is bubbling.

7. Remove pie from the oven and place on a wire rack to cool. Serve with whipped cream, if desired.

Serves 6 to 8

Chocolate Pie
with Pretzel Crust

I love chocolate covered pretzels! Yet I hadn't heard of using a pretzel crust until a few months ago. Intrigued, I made a pie. It was fantastic. The filling comes together very quickly. I make the pie before going to bed at night, so it will be waiting to be served the next day for dessert.

1 (14-ounce) bag gluten-free pretzels,
 finely crushed
3 tablespoons plus 3/4 cup granulated sugar
6 tablespoons butter, melted
1/2 teaspoon salt
1 (13-ounce) can evaporated milk
1 1/3 cups water

1/3 cup cornstarch
3 ounces unsweetened chocolate, chopped
2 teaspoons vanilla extract

Whipped cream, for serving (optional)

1. Preheat oven to 325°F. Combine pretzels, 3 tablespoons sugar, and butter in a medium bowl.

2. Press half of the mixture evenly onto the bottom and sides of a 9-inch pie pan.

3. Bake crust for 10 minutes or until lightly golden brown.

4. Remove crust from oven and place on a wire rack to cool.

5. In a medium saucepan combine remaining 3/4 cup sugar, salt, evaporated milk, water, and cornstarch; stir mixture vigorously with a fork to prevent the cornstarch from clumping. Heat mixture over medium heat, stirring constantly, until it reaches a boil and thickens.

6. Reduce heat to low and add chocolate. Stir quickly until chocolate melts. Remove pan from heat and stir in vanilla.

7. Pour filling into prepared crust.

8. Sprinkle remaining pretzel mixture onto hot filling.

9. Chill pie for at least 3 hours before serving. Serve with whipped cream, if desired.

Serves 6

Baker's Note

Gluten-free pretzels are very expensive! If making a crust with gluten-free pretzels doesn't fit in your budget, you can use a prebaked cookie crust (see recipe, page 187).

If you don't want to use a pretzel crust or a cookie crust, use a prebaked gluten-free piecrust. Prepare the dough for 1 piecrust (see recipe, page 187). Preheat oven to 425°F. Roll out the dough and line a 9-inch pie pan. Prick the bottom of the dough lightly with the tines of a fork. Bake for 10 to 12 minutes or until the crust is golden brown.

Buttermilk
Pie

Buttermilk pie always intrigued me, but for some reason I never got around to making one. When I finally did make one, I was thrilled with how easy it was to make. Whisk a few ingredients together, pour the filling into an unbaked piecrust and that's it! I had envisioned the cake being thick, almost like a cheesecake. I was wrong! The filling is creamy and lemony. It reminds me slightly of a lemon bar filling.

Dough for 1 single piecrust (see recipe, page 187)
2 cups buttermilk
2 large eggs
1 cup granulated sugar
2 tablespoons white rice flour

2 tablespoons cornstarch
2 tablespoons butter, melted
1/2 teaspoon grated lemon zest
Ground nutmeg, for sprinkling

1. Preheat oven to 425°F. Place a sheet of plastic wrap or parchment paper on a work surface and place half the dough on it; cover with another sheet of plastic or parchment. Roll out dough to a 12 1/2-inch circle and place into a 9-inch pie pan. Place pie pan on a baking sheet.

2. In a medium bowl, combine buttermilk, eggs, sugar, white rice flour, cornstarch, melted butter, and grated lemon zest. Whisk until smooth and thoroughly combined.

3. Pour filling into pie shell. Lightly sprinkle the top with nutmeg.

4. Place baking sheet and pie in oven and bake for 10 minutes. Reduce oven temperature to 325°F and bake for an additional 20 minutes, or until no filling clings to a tester gently inserted into the center of the pie.

5. Remove pie from oven and place on a wire rack to cool completely. Store pie in the refrigerator.

Serves 6 to 8

Piecrust
Cookies

After making a piecrust, why would you want to throw the leftover dough away? Make these great cookies. They are the ultimate cook's treat. You will notice there are no set measurements for the sugar and cinnamon. Use as much or as little as you like.

Leftover unbaked pie dough
Melted butter
Dark brown sugar
Cinnamon

1. Line a baking sheet with parchment paper. Roll out piecrust to 1/4 inch thick.

2. Brush dough generously with melted butter. Sprinkle evenly with brown sugar and cinnamon.

3. Roll piecrust into a log (think cinnamon buns).

4. Cut dough into 1/2-inch pieces.

5. Place cookies on prepared baking sheet.

6. Bake until golden brown. (Bake these cookies while your pie is in the oven; the oven should be set at 350°F.)

Yield will vary depending on how much pie dough you have left over

Oreos

Twinkies

Devil Dogs

Thin Mint Girl Scout–Style Cookies

Honey Maid Graham Crackers

Chocolate Graham Crackers

Animal Crackers

Tastes Like

Nabisco Old-Fashioned Ginger Snaps

Nabisco Nutter Butters

Nabisco Nilla Wafers

Girl Scout Samoas (Caramel De-Lites)

Nabisco Better Cheddars

Ritz Crackers

Premium Saltine Crackers

Oreos

This recipe goes together very quickly thanks to the food processor. Be sure to allow the dough to chill the dough for at least four hours or the oreos will not hold their round shape when baked. Also, the cookies need to be completely cooled before filling.

DRY INGREDIENTS

1 cup white rice flour

1/4 cup cornstarch

1/4 cup sweet rice flour

1/3 cup Dutch process cocoa powder

1/2 teaspoon baking powder

3/4 cup granulated sugar

1/8 teaspoon salt

WET INGREDIENTS

1/2 cup (1 stick) cold butter, cut into eight pieces

1 egg

2 tablespoons milk

Filling (see recipe, page 206)

1. In the bowl of a food processor, combine dry ingredients. Pulse to combine. Add the cold butter and pulse until no large pieces of butter remain. Add the egg and milk. Mix until a dough forms. (The dough should form a ball and "swirl" around the bowl of the food processor.) If dough is dry, add 1 to 2 teaspoons of milk and mix to form a dough.

2. Divide dough in half and pat each half into a round. Wrap each dough round tightly in plastic wrap. Chill dough for 4 hours or overnight.

3. Preheat oven to 350°F. Line two baking sheets with parchment paper. Set pan aside.

4. Remove dough from refrigerator. White rice flour your countertop and roll dough out to 1/8-inch thickness. (Remember, you will be sandwiching two cookies together. You don't want the individual cookies too thick.) Cut dough into rounds using a 11/2-inch cookie cutter. (If you have a fluted cookie cutter, use it. It will make the cookie look more like an Oreo.)

5. Place dough on prepared baking sheet, spacing the cookies about two inches apart. Bake for 10 to 12 minutes or until cookies are aromatic. (Cookies will look "dry" and smell very chocolaty.)

6. Transfer cookies to a wire rack to cool completely.

7. Fill using recipe on page 206.

Makes about 2 dozen sandwich cookies

Baker's Note

Store cookies in an airtight container to maintain a crisp texture.

Filling

4 tablespoons vegetable shortening (if you can't
  tolerate shortening, use 4 tablespoons butter)
2 cups confectioners' sugar
3 tablespoons water
1/2 teaspoon vanilla extract

1. In a small bowl, cream together all ingredients until smooth. (Use medium-high speed on handheld and stand mixers.) Mixture will be thick.

2. Spread the filling on half of the cooled cookies.

3. Top with the remaining cookies.

Twinkies

A few years ago, I wandered into a Williams-Sonoma store. Sitting proudly on display was a "cream boat" pan. This pan was for making homemade Twinkies! I knew many readers would love a recipe for gluten-free Twinkies, so I snatched up the pan. Apparently, I was one of the few people who thought making homemade Twinkies was a fabulous idea. The pan was quickly discontinued. I didn't want to frustrate people with the note, "If you happened to buy this pan the few weeks it was for sale, you're in luck. If you didn't, use a regular cake pan." My recipe for Twinkies could not run.

Then a few months ago, Twinkie-style pans began popping up at houseware stores like Bed, Bath, and Beyond. Now you, too, can make Twinkie-shape Twinkies!

Gluten-free nonstick cooking spray

DRY INGREDIENTS
1 1/4 cups white rice flour
1 cup cornstarch
1/4 cup sweet rice flour
1/2 teaspoon xanthan gum
3/4 teaspoon salt
2 1/2 teaspoons baking powder

WET INGREDIENTS
3/4 cup (1 1/2 sticks) butter, softened
1 3/4 cups granulated sugar
3 large eggs
2 large egg yolks
3/4 cup milk
2 teaspoons vanilla extract

Cream filling (see recipe, page 211)

1. Preheat oven to 350°F. Spray a cream boat pan lightly with cooking spray.

2. In a medium bowl, whisk together the dry ingredients.

3. In a large bowl, cream together butter and sugar until light and fluffy, about 45 seconds. (Use high speed on a handheld mixer or medium-high on a stand mixer.) Add the eggs and yolks to the butter mixture, 1 at a time, beating well after each addition. Add half of the dry ingredients and blend until combined. Add milk and vanilla. Blend for 45 seconds. Add remaining dry ingredients and blend until smooth.

4. Pour batter into prepared cake pan. Fill each cavity half way. Bake for about 20 minutes or until a tester inserted into the center of the cakes comes out clean.

5. Remove pan from oven and place pan on a wire rack to cool, 5 minutes. Turn cakes out onto the wire rack to cool completely.

6. Fit a piping bag with a round tip and fill with filling. Insert tip about 1 inch into the bottom of the cake. Squeeze the pastry bag while slowly withdrawing the tip. Repeat twice. (The finished cakes should have 3 holes each.) Flip cakes over so the smooth side is facing up.

Makes two dozen Twinkies

Baker's Note
The Twinkie pan is labeled as either a "cream boat" or "cream canoe" pan. The cavities on the pan look just like Twinkies, so no matter what the pan is called, you'll know it as soon as you see it.

Devil
Dogs

Devil dogs are made by Drake's Cakes and are available mostly in the Northeast. But that doesn't mean you haven't eaten something like a Devil Dog. Think chocolate snack cake.

Gluten-free nonstick cooking spray

DRY INGREDIENTS
1 1/2 cups white rice flour
1/2 cup cornstarch
1 cup sugar
1/4 teaspoon xanthan gum
1/2 cup cocoa powder
1 1/2 teaspoons baking soda
1/2 teaspoon salt

WET INGREDIENTS
1 cup milk
1/2 cup vegetable oil
2 teaspoons vanilla extract

Cream filling (see recipe, facing page)

1. Preheat oven to 350°F. Spray a cream boat pan lightly with cooking spray.

2. In a large bowl, whisk together dry ingredients. Add milk, vegetable oil, and vanilla. Blend until well combined. (Use medium-high speed on handheld and stand mixers.)

3. Spoon about 2 tablespoons batter into each cavity of the prepared baking pan.

4. Bake for 7 to 9 minutes or until a tester inserted into the center of the cakes comes out clean.

5. Remove pan from the oven and place pan on a wire rack to cool, 5 minutes. Turn cakes out onto the rack to cool completely.

6. Spread cream filling on half the cakes and top each with another cake.

Makes 16 Devil Dogs

Cream Filling

Use this filling for both the Twinkies and Devil Dogs.

1/2 cup (1 stick) butter, softened
1/4 cup vegetable shortening
3/4 cup confectioners' sugar
1 (7 1/2-ounce) jar marshmallow creme
1 teaspoon vanilla extract

1. In a medium bowl, cream together butter and vegetable shortening until light and fluffy. (Use high speed on a handheld mixer or medium-high on a stand mixer.) Add confectioners' sugar and blend until combined. Add marshmallow creme and vanilla; mix until fluffy.

Thin Mint
Girl Scout–Style Cookies

When I think of Girl Scout Cookies, I think of Thin Mints. The success of this recipe depends on the pure peppermint oil—not peppermint extract—used in the chocolate coating. The best part of making your own Thin Mint cookies is that you can make them all year long!

DRY INGREDIENTS

1 cup white rice flour

1/4 cup cornstarch

1/4 cup sweet rice flour

1/3 cup Dutch process cocoa powder

1/2 teaspoon baking powder

1/8 teaspoon salt

WET INGREDIENTS

1/2 cup (1 stick) butter, softened

3/4 cup sugar

1 large egg

2 tablespoons milk

Icing (see recipe, facing page)

1. In a medium bowl, whisk together the dry ingredients.

2. In a large bowl, cream together butter and sugar until light and fluffy. (Use medium-high speed on handheld and stand mixers.) Add egg and blend until well combined. Add dry ingredients and mix for 1 minute. Batter will be thick. Add milk and blend until incorporated.

3. Turn dough out onto a large piece of plastic wrap. Shape into a log about 1 1/2 inches in diameter. Wrap with plastic wrap and freeze at least 4 hours or overnight.

4. Preheat oven to 350°F. Line a baking sheet with parchment paper.

5. Remove plastic wrap from cookie log. Using a sharp knife, slice cookies into 1/4-inch slices. Place cookies about 1 inch apart on prepared baking sheet.

6. Bake for 10 minutes or until crisp.

7. Remove pan from the oven and place on a wire rack to cool, 3 to 5 minutes. Transfer cookies directly onto rack to cool completely.

8. Line a cookie sheet with parchment paper. Dip cookies into icing and place on parchment. Allow to harden.

Makes about 3 dozen cookies

Baker's Note

Chocolate needs to be treated gently! The best way to melt chocolate is in the microwave. Place your chocolate in a dry bowl. Water "seizes" chocolate. If any water is present the chocolate will not melt.

Icing

1/2 pound Merckens Dark Chocolate Coating
   or dark chocolate chips
3 to 4 drops pure peppermint oil
   (not peppermint extract)

1. Place the chocolate into a microwave-safe bowl and melt in a microwave. (Melt chocolate for 20 seconds, then remove the bowl from the microwave and stir. Repeat until completely melted.) Add peppermint oil and stir to combine.

Honey Maid
Graham Crackers

Scoring the dough with a pizza wheel prior to baking and pricking all over with a fork makes these graham crackers look just like store-bought graham crackers. Slightly sweet and pleasantly crunchy, these graham crackers can be eaten as is, made into s'mores, or ground into crumbs for a piecrust.

DRY INGREDIENTS

1 1/2 cups brown rice flour, plus more for dusting

1/2 cup cornstarch

1/3 cup packed dark brown sugar

1 teaspoon baking powder

1/2 teaspoon salt

WET INGREDIENTS

5 tablespoons cold butter

6 tablespoons milk

3 tablespoons honey

1. Preheat oven to 350°F. Place dry ingredients in the bowl of a food processor; pulse to combine. Add the butter; pulse until coarse. No large pieces of butter should remain. Add milk and honey. Pulse until a dough forms.

2. Place a 12x16-inch piece of parchment paper on a work surface; dust lightly with rice flour. Turn dough out onto parchment and pat into a rectangle. Dust the top of the dough lightly with rice flour. Place another piece of 12x16-inch parchment paper on top of the dough. Roll dough out until it covers all of the paper. Dough rectangle will be about 1/8 inch thick.

3. Carefully remove top piece of parchment paper. Transfer dough, with bottom parchment paper, to a 12x18-inch baking pan. Using a pizza wheel, score the dough into rectangles. (The rectangles should be 6x2 3/4 inches for standard graham crackers and 3x2 3/4 inches for s'more-size graham crackers.) Prick dough all over with a fork. Cover dough with plastic wrap and chill in the refrigerator for 10 minutes.

4. Bake for 15 minutes or until evenly brown.

5. Remove pan from the oven and place on a wire rack to cool, 3 to 5 minutes. Slide the parchment, with the crackers, directly onto the rack to cool completely. Break along scored lines.

Makes about 1 dozen graham crackers

Chocolate
Graham Crackers

DRY INGREDIENTS

1^1/2 cups brown rice flour, plus more for dusting

^{1}/4 cup cornstarch

^{1}/4 cup cocoa powder

^{1}/3 cup packed dark brown sugar

1 teaspoon baking powder

^{1}/2 teaspoon salt

WET INGREDIENTS

5 tablespoons cold butter

6 tablespoons milk

3 tablespoons light corn syrup

1. Preheat oven to 350°F. Place dry ingredients in the bowl of a food processor; pulse to combine. Add the butter. Pulse until mixture is coarse. No large pieces of butter should remain. Add milk and corn syrup. Pulse until a dough forms.

2. Place a 12-x-16-inch piece of parchment paper on a work surface and dust lightly with rice flour. Turn dough out onto parchment and pat into a rectangle. Dust the top of the dough lightly with rice flour. Place another piece of 12x16-inch parchment paper on top of the dough. Roll dough out until it covers all of the paper. Dough rectangle will be about ^{1}/8 inch thick.

3. Carefully remove top piece of parchment paper. Transfer dough, with bottom parchment paper, to a 12x18-inch baking pan. Using a pizza wheel, score the dough into rectangles. (The rectangles should be 6x2^3/4 inches for standard graham crackers and 3x2^3/4 for s'more-size graham crackers.) Prick dough all over with a fork. Cover dough with plastic wrap and place in the refrigerator to chill for 10 minutes.

4. Bake for 15 minutes or until evenly brown.

5. Remove pan from the oven and place on a wire rack to cool, 3 to 5 minutes. Slide the parchment, with the crackers, directly onto the rack to cool completely. Break along scored lines.

Makes about 1 dozen graham crackers

Animal Crackers

This recipe is based on the classic Barnum's Animal Crackers. Small animal cookie cutters can be found at cake decorating supply stores, so you can recreate your favorite shapes.

DRY INGREDIENTS

1 cup white rice flour, plus more for dusting

1/2 cup brown rice flour

1/2 cup cornstarch

1/2 cup granulated sugar

2 tablespoons dried sweet dairy whey

1 teaspoon baking powder

1/2 teaspoon salt

WET INGREDIENTS

1/2 cup (1 stick) cold butter

2 tablespoons light corn syrup

1/4 cup milk, plus more as needed

1 teaspoon lemon extract

1. In a large bowl, whisk together dry ingredients.

2. Using a pastry cutter or fork, cut butter into dry ingredients until no large pieces of butter remain. Add corn syrup, milk, and lemon flavoring. Stir together until a dough forms. (If dough is dry add a few teaspoons additional milk.)

3. Divide dough in half and pat into 2 disks. Wrap disks tightly with plastic wrap and refrigerate overnight.

4. Preheat oven to 375°F. Line a baking sheet with parchment paper.

5. Remove dough from the refrigerator and allow it to sit on the counter for 10 minutes.

6. Lightly dust a work surface with white rice flour. Roll out dough, about 1/8 inch thick, and cut into desired shapes.

7. Place cookies on prepared baking sheet. Bake 8 to 12 minutes or until golden brown.

8. Remove baking sheet from oven and place on a wire rack to cool, 3 to 5 minutes. Transfer crackers directly onto rack to cool completely.

Yield will vary depending on the size of the cutters you use

Nabisco Old-Fashioned Ginger Snaps

With their hard texture and pungent ginger flavor, these cookies look and taste just like Nabisco's original.

DRY INGREDIENTS

1 3/4 cups white rice flour

1/4 cup cornstarch

1/4 cup sweet rice flour

2 teaspoons baking soda

1/2 teaspoon salt

1 tablespoon ground ginger

1 teaspoon ground cinnamon

1/2 teaspoon ground nutmeg

1/4 teaspoon xanthan gum

WET INGREDIENTS

1 cup packed dark brown sugar

3/4 cup vegetable shortening

1 large egg

1/4 cup unsulphered molasses

1. Preheat oven to 350°F. Line 2 baking sheets with parchment paper.

2. In a medium bowl, whisk together dry ingredients.

3. In a large bowl, cream together brown sugar and vegetable shortening for 30 seconds. (Use high speed on a handheld mixer or medium-high on a stand mixer.) Add egg and mix for 30 seconds. Add dry ingredients and molasses; blend until a dough forms, about 1 minute. (Use medium speed on both a handheld mixer and stand mixer.)

4. Roll dough into 2-teaspoon balls. Place dough balls 2 inches apart on prepared baking sheets and flatten slightly using your palm.

5. Bake first sheet of cookies for 10 to 12 minutes or until cookies are golden brown and aromatic.

6. Remove cookie sheet from oven and place on wire racks to cool, 3 to 5 minutes. Transfer cookies directly onto racks to cool completely. While first sheet is cooking, bake second sheet of cookies.

Makes about 5 dozen cookies

Nabisco
Nutter Butters

While developing this recipe, I hit a bit of a wall. Classic Nabisco Nutter Butter cookies are shaped like a peanut, but no one makes a peanut-shaped cookie cutter. Therefore, this recipe tastes just like a Nabisco Nutter Butter, but it doesn't look like one. As soon as they make a peanut cutter—and you know they will eventually—you can cut the dough out with one of those. For now, use a round cutter.

DRY INGREDIENTS

1/2 cup white rice flour, plus more for dusting

1/4 cup cornstarch

1/4 cup sweet rice flour

1/2 cup gluten-free oats, ground into a fine flour in food processor

1/2 teaspoon salt

1/4 teaspoon xanthan gum

WET INGREDIENTS

1/2 cup vegetable shortening

3 tablespoons creamy peanut butter (not natural peanut butter)

2/3 cup granulated sugar

1 large egg

Filling (see recipe, facing page)

1. Preheat oven to 350°F. Line 2 baking sheets with parchment paper.

2. In a medium bowl, whisk together dry ingredients.

3. In a large bowl, cream together vegetable shortening, peanut butter, and sugar. Cream for 30 seconds. (Use high speed on a handheld mixer or medium-high on a stand mixer.) Add the egg and mix 15 seconds. Scrape down the sides of the bowl and mix 15 seconds. Reduce mixer speed to medium-low and add dry ingredients; mix until a dough forms.

4. Chill dough for 10 minutes.

5. Dust a work surface lightly with white rice flour. Roll out half the dough to about 1/4 inch thick. Cut out dough with a 3-inch round cookie cutters and transfer to prepared baking sheets. Repeat with remaining dough.

6. Bake first sheet of cookies for 8 to 10 minutes or until cookies are lightly brown.

7. Remove pan from oven and set on a wire rack to cool, 3 to 5 minutes. Transfer cookies directly onto rack to cool completely. While first sheet is cooling, bake second sheet of cookies.

8. Sandwich cookies together with a thin layer of filling.

Makes 2 dozen cookies

Filling

1/2 cup creamy peanut butter (not natural
    peanut butter)
3/4 cup confectioners' sugar

1. In a small bowl, combine peanut butter and confectioners' sugar. Blend until smooth.
(Use medium-high speed on handheld and stand mixers.)

Nabisco
Nilla Wafers

Not only does this recipe make great Nilla Wafers for eating out of hand, you can also use these cookies as a great base for banana pudding!

DRY INGREDIENTS
1/2 cup white rice flour
1/4 cup cornstarch
1/4 teaspoon baking powder
1/4 teaspoon xanthan gum
1/2 teaspoon salt

WET INGREDIENTS
1/4 cup (1/2 stick) butter, softened
1/2 cup granulated sugar
1 large egg
1 large egg white
1/2 teaspoon lemon extract
1 teaspoon vanilla extract
2 tablespoons vegetable oil

1. Preheat oven to 350°F. Line 2 baking sheets with parchment paper.

2. In a small bowl, whisk together dry ingredients.

3. In a medium bowl, combine butter and sugar; mix for 30 seconds. (Use high speed on a handheld mixer or medium-high speed on a stand mixer.) Add egg, egg white, lemon extract, vanilla, and oil. Mix for 15 seconds. Batter will be thin.

4. Using a teaspoon, drop batter onto prepared baking sheets, spacing cookies 2 inches apart.

5. Bake first sheet of cookies for 10 to 12 minutes or until cookies are golden brown.

6. Remove cookie sheet from oven and set on wire racks to cool, 3 to 5 minutes. Transfer cookies directly onto racks to cool completely. While first sheet is cooling, bake second sheet of cookies.

Makes about 10 dozen cookies

Girl Scout Samoas (Caramel De-Lites)

Rich with caramel, coconut, and chocolate, these cookies are almost like a piece of candy. Be sure to use Mercken's block caramel and unsweetened coconut. After many trial recipes, I found that other brands of caramel were too hard and broke the cookie. Regular sweetened coconut has the wrong texture and taste for a perfect Samoa.

1/2 recipe Nabisco-style Nilla Wafers, baked and
   cooled (see recipe, page 220)
1 pound Mercken's soft caramel
1/2 cup unsweetened coconut
1 pound dark chocolate, melted (Merckens Dark
   Chocolate Coating)

1. Line a baking sheet with parchment paper.

2. Press 1/2 teaspoon caramel on the top of each cookie. Place caramel-coated cookies onto prepared baking sheet.

3. Once all cookies are covered with caramel, melt the chocolate in a small microwave-safe bowl. (Microwave chocolate for 20 seconds, then remove the bowl from the microwave and stir. Repeat until completely melted.)

4. Stir in coconut. Use a fork to dip each cookie into the melted chocolate, lightly tapping the fork on the edge of the bowl to remove excess chocolate. (If chocolate begins to harden while you are working, simply re-melt it in the microwave.)

5. Place dipped cookie on prepared baking sheet to harden.

Makes about 5 dozen cookies

Nabisco
Better Cheddars

Like spice? Sprinkle the crackers with chili powder and kosher salt before baking for a spicy treat.

2 cups freshly grated sharp yellow cheddar cheese
1 1/2 cups white rice flour, plus more for dusting
1/2 cup cornstarch
1/4 cup (1/2 stick) butter, softened

1 teaspoon xanthan gum
1/2 cup cold water
Kosher salt, for sprinkling

1. Place cheese, rice flour, cornstarch, butter, and xanthan gum in the bowl of a food processor; pulse 3 or 4 times to combine. Add the water and pulse another 3 to 4 times to form a thick dough.

2. Dust a work surface with rice flour. Turn dough out onto prepared surface. Divide dough in half and roll each half into a log about 1 1/2 inches in diameter. Wrap the logs tightly in plastic wrap and chill for 2 hours or overnight.

3. Preheat oven to 425°F. Line 2 baking sheets with parchment paper.

4. Remove dough from the refrigerator. Using a sharp knife, slice the dough very thin, about 1/16 of an inch. Place dough rounds on the prepared baking sheets. Sprinkle the tops of the crackers lightly with kosher salt. Prick the tops a few times each with a fork.

5. Bake first sheet of crackers for about 5 minutes or until aromatic and golden brown.

6. Remove sheet from the oven and place on wire racks to cool, 3 to 5 minutes. Transfer crackers directly onto racks to cool completely. While first sheet is cooling, bake second sheet of crackers.

Makes about 4 1/2 dozen crackers

Baker's Note
The two keys to this recipe are chilling the dough and slicing it thin. If you don't chill the dough, you will end up with crackers that spread and are tough. And if the slices are too thick, the crackers won't crunch.

Ritz Crackers

DRY INGREDIENTS

1 1/4 cups white rice flour, plus more for dusting

1/2 cup cornstarch

1/4 cup sweet rice flour

1 teaspoon salt

1 teaspoon baking powder

1/2 teaspoon xanthan gum

2 1/2 tablespoons granulated sugar

WET INGREDIENTS

1/4 cup (1/2 stick) cold butter, cut into
   1/4-inch pieces

1 large egg

6 tablespoons heavy cream

3 tablespoons butter, melted, for the tops of
   the crackers

Kosher salt, for sprinkling

1. In a large bowl, whisk together dry ingredients.

2. Using your fingers or a pastry cutter, cut in chilled butter until mixture resembles a coarse meal. (No large pieces of butter should remain.)

3. In a separate bowl, mix together egg and cream until smooth. Pour the egg mixture over the dry ingredients. Stir with a fork until dough forms a loose ball.

4. Using your hands, gather the dough together and pat into a disk, about 1 inch thick. Wrap the dough in plastic wrap and chill for 1 1/2 hours or overnight.

5. Preheat oven to 425°F. Line 2 baking sheets with parchment paper. Dust a work surface lightly with rice flour. Roll dough out to about a 1/8-inch thickness. Using a 3-inch round cookie cutter, cut the dough into circles. Place circles on prepared baking sheets. Prick circles all over with a fork. Press dough scraps together and repeat until you've used all the dough.

6. Bake first sheet of crackers for 6 minutes. Remove the pan from the oven, and carefully turn crackers over. Bake crackers for an additional 4 to 5 minutes or until golden brown.

7. Remove crackers from oven and lightly brush with melted butter. Immediately sprinkle kosher salt over the tops of the crackers. Transfer crackers to a wire rack to cool completely. While first sheet cools, bake second sheet of crackers.

Makes about 3 1/2 dozen crackers

Premium Saltine Crackers

DRY INGREDIENTS

1 cup white rice flour

1/2 cup brown rice flour

1/2 cup cornstarch

1 1/2 teaspoons baking powder

1/2 teaspoon xanthan gum

3/4 teaspoon salt

WET INGREDIENTS

6 tablespoons cold butter, cut into small pieces

1/2 cup cold water

Kosher salt, for sprinkling

1. Preheat oven to 425°F. In a large mixing bowl, combine dry ingredients. Add cold butter. Blend, using medium speed on handheld and stand mixers, until butter is cut into the dough and no large pieces of butter remain. When correctly mixed, dry ingredients should resemble lumpy sand; some pea-size pieces of butter will remain. Add water and blend until a dough forms.

2. Place a 12x16-inch piece of parchment paper on a work surface. Place dough on parchment paper and cover with another 12x16-inch piece of parchment. Roll dough incredibly thin, about 1/16 inch. When you think the dough is thin enough, roll it a little more. The dough will cover about two-thirds of the parchment paper. Remove top piece of parchment paper. Prick the dough all over with a fork. Using a pizza wheel, cut the dough into cracker-size pieces. Generously sprinkle kosher salt all over the top of the dough.

3. Carefully transfer parchment paper with dough to a baking sheet. Bake for 20 to 25 minutes or until the crackers are golden brown.

4. Remove pan from the oven. Pull parchment paper onto a wire rack and allow crackers to cool completely.

Makes about 2 dozen crackers

Index

C